OUTLINES OF JAINISM

OUTLINES OF JAINISM

S. GOPALAN
Centre of Advanced Study in Philosophy
University of Madras

HALSTED PRESS
A Division of JOHN WILEY & SONS, Inc.,
605 Third Avenue, New York, N.Y. 10016

ISBN 0 85226 324 4

Published by Virendra J. Majumdar for Wiley Eastern Private Limited,
J 43A South Extension 1, New Delhi 110049 and printed
at Prominent Printers, Naveen Shahdara, Delhi 32

Contents

Preface

THE book was born out of the course I have been offering on Jainism in the Centre of Advanced Study in Philosophy, University of Madras, since 1969. The course leading to the Master's Degree in Indian Philosophy of the University of Madras has had an international composition and hence it required not merely 'the statement of facts' about the Jaina tradition but it involved, more basically, situating Jainism as an integral aspect of Indian tradition. In the course of my lectures my endeavour has been to show that a true understanding of Jainism would be possible only if it is considered in the light of Indian tradition as a whole, and also to maintain that the richness of Indian culture could be appreciated better by delving deep into the various aspects of the Jaina philosophy. This meant primarily that I had to 'dissect out' the Jaina tradition and analyse its various facets in detail, in addition to clearing the misunderstanding about its origin and relationship with sister-systems.

At the instance of my students I reduced my whole analysis to writing and I thought it would be better, both from the point of view of the lay reader — both Indian and foreign — and from the point of view of serious scholars of Jaina thought, to take a comprehensive sweep of the whole tradition and at the same time observe brevity in treating the essentials of the subject. The sections dealing with a general introduction to Jainism, epistemology, psychology, metaphysics and ethics have hence been designed with this aim in view. It is realised that the comprehensive vision and the depth of understanding that are characteristic of the Jaina philosophers do not justify spanning the tradition within a meagre two hundred pages, but it is hoped that a proper understanding of the spirit of the tradition can well be promoted by treating (however briefly) important aspects of it not merely with the intention of offering an exposition of the subject-matter but with the idea of working out a proper interpretative approach to the whole tradition. Rather than claiming that interpretation is the key-characteristic of the present work I submit that my prime concern in the book has been to maintain that if we can deftly remove the sheath of ordinary understanding of the tradition by getting an access to the spirit behind the concepts, the significance of Jainism as a whole can well be grasped. A few pages on the Anuvrata movement, inaugurated by the living Jaina saint Acarya Tulasi, it is hoped, will illustratively signify that the age-old Jaina concepts can still be revived and made meaningful in the context of the contemporary situation.

I must record here my thanks to my students who by their innocent curiosity and earnest desire to deeply understand the tradition stimulated my own thinking and made possible the writing of the book. My thanks are also due to the publishers who evinced a keen interest in bringing out the book and for expeditiously executing the work. Before concluding let me record here my deep appreciation of the pains which my wife Uma took to help me while I was editing the book and especially for the preparation of the Index and the Bibliography.

May 26, 1973

Centre of Advanced Study in Philosophy, S. GOPALAN
University of Madras, Madras 5

PART I
INTRODUCTION

1

Is Jainism an Offshoot of Buddhism ?

IT is well-known that of the three major religions of India, viz., Hinduism, Buddhism and Jainism only the first two have attracted the attention of scholars, Indian as well as Western, and that Jainism, as a subject of study, has been neglected even by Indian scholars. It is indeed amazing how, Jainism, though it is still a living religion in India, has been virtually overlooked even in the country of its origin, whereas Buddhism, which has more or less disappeared from the Indian soil, has been seriously studied in India and more widely understood than its sister-faith Jainism. One reason for this predicament may be that Buddhism was so influential at one time that it was considered *the religion of Asia.* Surendranath Dasgupta adduces two reasons for the exaggerated importance accorded to Buddhism : (1) some resemblances between the two religions which seem to be striking (though not really decisive) and (2) inability of scholars — both foreign and Indian — to have direct access to the Jaina source-books. He writes : "Notwithstanding the radical differences in their philosophical notions Jainism and Buddhism which were originally both orders of monks outside the pale of Brahmanism, present some resemblances in outward appearance,and some European scholars who became acquainted with Jainism through inadequate samples of Jaina literature easily persuaded themselves that it was an offshoot of Buddhism, and even Indians unacquainted with Jaina literature are often found to commit the same mistake."[1]

[1] *A History of Indian Philosophy* (Cambridge : University Press, 1963), Vol. I, p. 169

The resemblances he has in mind here are probably the following : (1) both the religions originated in the same part of India (2) both were opposed to the orthodox views that prevailed in the country at that time (3) both were against the caste structure of the Hindu society (4) both have denounced the idea of a personal god (*Īśvara*) in their respective systems (5) both make use of identical terms, though with different connotations and (6) both have accorded greater importance to the concept and practice of non-injury (*ahiṁsā*) than even Hinduism.

The wrong understanding that results when a scholar scans through some translations of classical texts in order to find support for his own point of view is not a situation peculiar to Indian thought and it requires no elaboration here. That Jainism has been considered, even by the academic world, as a mere offshoot of Buddhism requires to be noticed here. W.S. Lilly writes : "Buddhism in proper survives in the land of its birth in the form of Jainism. What is certain is that Jainism came into notice when Buddhism had disappeared from India."[2] H. H. Wilson even goes to the extent of maintaining that Jainism came into existence only during the 8th or 9th century A.D. He observes : "From all credible testimony, therefore, it is impossible to avoid the inference that the Jainas are a sect of comparatively recent institution who came into power and patronage about the 8th and 9th century : they probably existed before that date as a division of the Bauddhas, and owed their elevation to the suppression of that form of faith to which they contributed. This is positively asserted by the traditions of the south in several instances : the Bauddhas of Kanchi were confuted by Akalanka, a Jain priest, and thereupon expelled from the country. Vara Pandya of Madura, on becoming a Jain, is said to have persecuted the Bauddhas, subjecting them to personal tortures, and banishing them from the country. . .There is every reason to be satisfied, therefore, that the total disappearance of the Bauddhas in India proper is connected with the influence of the Jains which may have commenced in the sixth or seventh centuries and continued till the twelfth."[3] Sir Charles Eliot maintains : "Many of their doctrines especially their disregard not only of priests but of gods, which

[2] Cited by C.J. Shah, *Jainism in North India* (London : Longman Green & Co., 1932), Intr., p. xviii

[3] *Works of Wilson* (London : Trubner & Co., 1861), Vol. I, p. 334

seems to us so strange in any system which can be called a religion, are closely analogous to Buddhism and from one point of view Jainism is a part of the Buddhist movement. But more accurately it may be called an early specialized form of the general movement which culminated in Buddhism."[4]

Thanks to the researches of two German scholars Jainism is no longer considered to be a mere offshoot of Buddhism. Hermann Jacobi, in his introduction to his edition of *Kalpa-Sūtra*[5] and his paper *Mahāvīra and his Predecessors*[6] showed that Jainism had an independent origin. George Bühler gave a scientific and comprehensive account of the birth and growth of Jainism in his article *The Indian Sect of the Jainas.*[7]

It is quite possible that since the twenty-fourth Tīrthaṅkara, Mahāvīra (who is mistakenly considered to be the founder of Jainism) is referred to by some other names in the Jaina and Buddhist classics, researchers have not been able to appreciate the fact that Jainism, far from being an offshoot of Buddhism, had, in fact, an earlier origin. Mahāvīra belonged to *Jñātri-kṣatriya* class and so was known as *Jñātriputra*. The Jainas in general were referred to in Saṁskrit classics as *Nirgranthas* (those who have been freed from the fetters) and in the Pāli classics of Buddhism as *Nigaṇṭhas.* A reference to the latter is particularly illuminating as it lays bare facts not so clearly evident nor well-known to casual students of Jainism. The Pāli equivalent of *jñāta* is *nāta* and hence in the Buddhist classics Mahāvīra is referred to as Nātaputta. The Buddhist *Piṭakas* refer to the *Nigaṇṭhas* as opponents of the Buddha and his followers. No doubt, the reference is for the sake of refuting the rival doctrines. The terms *Nigaṇṭhanātha*, *Nigaṇṭha Nātaputta* and *Nātaputta* that are found in the Buddhist texts refer to Mahāvīra. Regarding this Bühler writes : "The discovery of the real name of the founder of the Jainas[8] belongs to Professor Jacobi and myself. The form

[4] *Hinduism and Buddhism* (London : Routledge & Kegan Paul Ltd., 1962), Vol. I, p. 105

[5] *The Kalpa-Sūtra of Bhadrabāhu* (Leipzig, 1879), pp. 1-15

[6] See *The Indian Antiquary*, Vol. IX, pp. 158 ff.

[7] Paper read in 1877

[8] It will be noticed here that Mahāvīra is referred to as the founder of the Jaina tradition. Such a reference must indeed have been a slip from the learned scholar's pen.

Jñātriputra occurs in the Jaina and northern Buddhist books; in Pāli it is *Nātaputta*, and in Jain Prākṛt *Nayaputta*. *Jñāta* or *Jñāti* appears to have been the name of the Rajput clan from which the *Nirgrantha* was descended."[9] From the fact that in these Buddhist sources the bare name of Mahāvīra alone is not referred to, but with the name of the philosophical school to which he belonged, it is evident that Jainism was in existence even before the time of Mahāvīra. It is not disputed that the Buddha and Mahāvīra were contemporaries and since the Buddhist classics refer to the Jaina school of thought it can be concluded that Jainism was an independent religion having its roots in an earlier epoch. An old Buddhist canon, *Sāmagāma Sutta* refers to the death of a *nigaṇṭha* — *Nātaputta* in Pāvā. Another Buddhist text *Magghima Nikāya* refers to a dispute between the Buddha and a son of a *nigaṇṭha.* The mention, in the Buddhist texts, of the Jainas as a class re-affirms the view that they were certainly not a sub-class under the Buddhists.

Moreover, the Buddhist texts nowhere point out that the *nigaṇṭhas* were a newly founded sect. So Jainism must have existed for a considerable time before the Buddha. Jacobi observes: "The *Nirgranthas* are frequently mentioned by the Buddhists even in the oldest part of the *Piṭakas*. But I have not yet met with a distinct mention of the Bauddhas in any of the old Jaina *Sūtras*, though they contain lengthy legends about Jamāli, Gośāla and other heterodox teachers. As this is just the reverse position to that which both sects mutually occupy in all aftertimes, and as it is inconsistent with our assumption of a contemporaneous origin of both creeds, we are driven to the conclusion that the *Nirgranthas* were not a newly founded sect of Buddha's time. This seems to have been the opinion of the *Piṭakas* too; for we find no indication of the contrary in them."[10] This lends support to our surmise that Jainism was in existence before the Buddha and Mahāvīra.

Another significant contributory factor to our position regarding the antiquity of Jainism is to be found in the sixfold classification of humanity by Gośāla, a contemporary of the Buddha and Mahāvīra. One of the classes he mentions is that of the *Nigaṇṭhas*. Had Jainism come into existence just then Gośāla would certainly not have regarded the *Nigaṇṭhas* as a dominant division of mankind.

[9] *I.A.*, VII, p. 143
[10] *I.A.*, IX, p. 161

Jacobi refers to another important point in this connection. He attributes the confusion regarding Jainism to the fact that certain common terms are used in Jainism and Buddhism. The names and appellations used for both were : *Jīna*, *Arhat*, *Mahāvīra Savajña*, *Sugata*, *Tathāgata*, *Siddha*, *Buddha*, *Sambuddha*, *Mukta* etc., though only a few of these were used to refer to the 24th Tīrthaṅkara of the Jaina tradition, and certain others to the founder of Buddhism.

The inference drawn is that the Jainas borrowed the terms from the Buddhists. Jacobi argues that the inference is unwarranted. If the titles bore a particular significance or acquired some special meaning beyond the one warranted by etymology, they could either have been adopted or rejected. He maintains that it is impossible that a word which had acquired some special meaning (in our context, in the hands of the Buddhists) should have been adopted but used in the original sense by the borrowers (Jainas).[11]

Jacobi emphasizes that the *only* inference that can be drawn is that there was and is at all times a number of honorific adjectives and substantives applicable to persons of exalted virtue; and that these words were used as epithets in their original meaning by all sects but some were selected as titles for their prophets — the choice being determined either by the fitness of the word itself or by other circumstances. Thus the only valid conclusion that can be drawn from the common terminology adopted by Jainism and Buddhism is that the Jainas and Buddhists were opposed to each other in regard to adoption of terminology.[12]

Another resemblance between the two religions has also been pointed out in favour of the contention that the Jainas 'imitated' the Buddhists. The followers of both the religions erect statues of their prophets in their temples and offer worship. In this connection it should be noted that the erection of statues was perfectly in accord with the Jaina teaching whereas it was *not* in keeping with the spirit of Buddhism. So, if at all, the Buddhists might have borrowed the practice from the Jainas and not vice versa.

To be fair to the Buddhists, however, it should be conceded that worshipping of prophets did not have anything to do with their religion in its original form just as Jainism in its pure form did not

[11] *Jaina Sūtras*, trans., (Delhi : Motilal Banarsidass, 1964), pt. I, Intr., pp. xix-xx

[12] *Ibid.*, Intr., pp. xx-xxi

countenance the worshipping of mortal forms. In this connection Jacobi points out that rather than referring to the worshipping of prophets to account for the origin of either Jainism or Buddhism it is more logical and true to facts to point to the higher religious consciousness of the Indian people. He opines that the people in general felt the need for a higher cult than that of their rude deities and demons and the religious development of India found in *bhakti* the supreme means of salvation. Therefore instead of seeing in the Buddhists the originals and in the Jainas the imitators it is more reasonable to assume that both sects independently of each other adopted this practice by the perpetual and irresistible influence of the religious development of the Indian people.[13] The practice itself is attributable to the lay followers of both the religions and in this the strong religious consciousness of the Indian people must have played a dominant role.

It is heartening for us to find support for our view in Dasgupta who observes : "The pioneers of this new system probably drew their suggestions from the sacrificial creed and from the Upaniṣads, and built their systems independently by their own rational thinking."[14] Jacobi also maintains : "Buddhism and Jainism must be regarded as religions developed out of Brahmanism, not by sudden reformation, but prepared by a religious movement going on for a long time."[15] It is interesting to notice that a scholar like Eliot, who is more sympathetic to Buddhism than to Jainism endorses the view that both the heterodox systems must have had their roots in the Brahmanic religion. It is significant that in the process of explaining the origin of Jainism and Buddhism he concedes the earlier origin of Jainism, though he speaks in high praise of the sister-faith, Buddhism. He writes : "Both are offshoots of a movement which was active in India in the 6th century B.C. in certain districts and especially among the aristocracy. Of these offshoots—the survivors among many which had hardly outlived their birth—Jainism was a trifle the earlier, but Buddhism was superior and more satisfying to the intellect and moral sense alike. Out of the theory and practice of religious life current in their time Gotama fashioned

[13] *Ibid.*, Intr., p. xi
[14] *op.* cit., Vol. I, p. 120
[15] *Jaina Sūtras*, pt. I, Intr., p. xxxii

a beautiful vase, Mahāvīra, a homely but still durable pot."[16]

Weber points to the striking similarities between the five great vows of the Jainas and the five cardinal virtues of the Buddhists. Similarly Windisch compares the *mahāvratas* of the Jainas with the 'ten obligations' of the Buddhists. From the similarities pointed out it may be agreed that one sect might have borrowers from the other but it is hard to determine whether the borrowed were the Jainas or the Buddhists.

Similarity in regard to the measurement of the history of the world found in the two religions is sometimes pointed to in support of the contention that Jainism was modelled on Buddhism. But even a little reflection will show that this might not have been the case. The Jainas talk in terms of *utsarpiṇī* and *avasarpiṇī* with the six Aras. It is impossible to derive this division of time from the Buddhists who had a conception of four great *kalpas* and eighty smaller *kalpas*. The Buddhists might have had as their model the *yugas* and *kalpas* of the Brahmanic Hinduism. The Jainas might have been influenced by the Hindu mythological belief of the day and night of Brahma constituting the eras of mankind. In any case Buddhism does not seem to have influenced the Jaina division of time.

The possibility that both the religions borrowed the ideas from the Hindus can't be ruled out completely. For instance the *Baudhāyana Dharma Sūtra* prescribes the following vows : abstention from injuring living beings, truthfulness, abstention from appropriating the property of others, continence and liberality. The first four great vows agree with those of the Jaina ascetics and are mentioned in the same order. The Buddhists also have the same virtues prescribed for their monks, though truthfulness is not given the second place in their list. Max Müller, Bühler and Kern hold this view and they have compared in detail the ascetic practices found in the three great religions and arrived at this conclusion.

The striking resemblance between the Hindu concept of *saṁnyāsa* or the rules prescribed for the ascetic and for the Jaina and Bauddha *bhikshus* points to the fact that there is no reason to believe that the Jainas imitated the Buddhists in framing the rules and

[16] *op. cit.*, Vol. I, pp. 122-123

regulations for their monks. The similarity that characterizes the rules for the ascetic in the Hindu and the Jaina traditions on the one hand, and the differences discernible in the rules prescribed for the Hindu *saṁnyāsin* and the Buddhist monk on the other, are evidences enough to establish our contention that Jainism was not a mere offshoot of Buddhism. We shall cite here the remarkable similarities between the rules governing the institution of asceticism in the Hindu and Jaina traditions. Since there is no dispute regarding the antiquity of Hindu thought, and since the Buddha is considered to be the founder of Buddhism and a contemporary of Mahāvīra who was only a reformer of the Jaina church scholars have come to the conclusion that if at all we are to refer to 'borrowal', it must be that Jainism and Buddhism 'borrowed' ideas from Hinduism, and not certainly Jainism from Buddhism. The following are some of the rules prescribed for the ascetic :

"An ascetic shall not possess any store."[17] In Jainism and Buddhism also we find the monks being forbidden to possess anything which can be called 'their own'.

"He must be chaste."[18] The fourth *mahāvrata* of the Jaina *muni* is exactly the same. This virtue is numbered five in the Buddhist list.

"He must not change his residence during the rainy season."[19] We find the same rule in the other two traditions also.

"He shall restrain his speech, his eyes and his actions."[20] We are here reminded of the three *guptis* of the Jainas.

"He shall not take parts of plants and trees except such as have become detached spontaneously."[21] The spirit of this rule is found reflected in the Jaina tradition which allows the *muni* to eat only such vegetables, fruits, etc. which have no trace of life left.[22]

"He shall avoid the destruction of seeds."[23] The Jaina tradition applies the rule to all living creatures when it exhorts its

[17] *Gautama* : III. 11; Cf. *Baudhāyana* : II, 6, 11, 16
[18] *Gautama* : III. 12
[19] *Ibid* , III. 13; Cf. *Baudhāyana* : II, 6, 11, 20
[20] *Ibid.,* III. 17
[21] *Ibid.*, III. 20
[22] *Ācārāṅga*, II. 1. 7. 6
[23] *Gautama* : III. 23

adherents to carefully avoid injuring eggs, living beings, seeds, sprouts, etc.

"He shall be indifferent towards all creatures, whether they do him an injury or a kindness."[24] Acceptance of this spirit of non-attachment in the Jaina tradition is evident from the description of Mahāvīra : "More than four months many sorts of living beings gathered on his body, crawled about it and caused pain."[25]

"He shall carry a cloth for straining water for the sake of purification."[26]

Before concluding we may refer to an instance of a scholar revising his opinion about Jainism after a deeper study. Washburn Hopkins who was extremely critical about Jainism initially wrote that of all the great religious sects of India that of Nātaputta is the least interesting, and has the least excuse to exist, for its chief points are that one should deny god, worship man and nourish vermin. He later regretted his improper understanding of Jainism. In a letter to Sri Vijaya Suri he wrote : "I found at once that the practical religion of the Jainas was one worthy of all commendation, and I have since regretted that I stigmatized the Jaina religion as insisting on denying God, worshipping man and nourishing vermin as its chief tenets without giving regard to the wonderful effect this religion has on the character and morality of the people. But as is often the case, a close acquaintance with a religion brings out its good side and creates a much more favourable impression of it as a whole than can be obtained by an objective literary acquaintance."[27]

It can therefore be maintained that an objective consideration of the history of Jainism lends no countenance to the view that Jainism branched off from Buddhism and launched on an independent career. We have endeavoured to show that even in the absence of historically unchallenged evidences to the antiquity of Jainism, — putting it back to the time of origin of mankind —, the earlier origin of Jainism has to be conceded and that it was not a mere branch of Buddhism.

[24] *Gautama* : III. 24
[25] *Ācārāṅga*, I. 8. 1. 2
[26] *Baudhāyana* : II, 6, 11, 14
[27] Cited by C. J. Shah, *op. cit.*, Intr., pp. xix-xx

2

Jainism Before Mahavira

ONE of the misunderstandings regarding Jainism is that Mahāvīra was its founder. Serious students have taken pains to show that though it is difficult to assign a specific date for the origin of Jainism, it is a historical fact that Jainism was older than Mahāvīra. C.J. Shah writes : "It is really difficult, nay impossible, to fix a date for the origin of Jainism. Nevertheless modern research has brought us at least to that stage wherein we can boldly proclaim all those worn-out theories about Jainism being a later offshoot of Buddhism or Brahmanism as gross ignorance or....as erroneous misstatements. On the other hand we have progressed a step further, and it would be now considered an historical fallacy to say that Jainism originated with Mahāvīra without putting forth any new grounds for justifying this statement. This is because it is now a recognized fact that Pārśva, the twenty-third Tīrthaṅkara of the Jainas, is an historical person, and Mahāvīra, like any other *jīna*, enjoyed no better position than that of a reformer in the galaxy of the Tīrthaṅkaras of the Jainas."[1]

It is clear from the above that if Mahāvīra is considered to have originated Jainism it will be difficult for us to account for its hoary past. The Jainas claim that their religion is eternal and that during every *yuga* it has been revealed by twenty-four Tīrthaṅkaras. Of the present age the first Tīrthaṅkara is considered to be one Ṛṣabha and the last, Mahāvīra.[2] So Mahāvīra can, according to

[1] *op. cit.*, p. 2

[2] The other twenty-two Tīrthaṅkaras (from the second to the twenty-third)

the Jaina tradition, be considered to be one of the reformers who were responsible for revitalizing and reinterpreting certain moral principles when humanity began treading the unrighteous path.

In the Jaina canons we find a mention by name of all the twenty-four Tīrthaṅkaras in the order in which they appeared and about their life-span. Ṛṣabha, the first Tīrthaṅkara is believed to have lived for 8,400,000 years,[3] the twenty-second Tīrthaṅkara, Nemi, for 1000 years, the twenty-third Tīrthaṅkara, Pārśva, for 100 years and the twenty-fourth Tīrthaṅkara, Mahāvīra, for 72 years.[4]

Though Jacobi and some other scholars believe that there must be something historical even about the first of the Tīrthaṅkaras, and though the Jainas consider the *Pūrvas*, the oldest of their sacred books as dating back to Ṛṣabha, scholars confirm the *historicity of the last two Tīrthaṅkaras alone*, i.e., of Pārśva and Mahāvīra. For instance Lassen writes of Pārśva : "That this *jīna* was a real person is specially supported by the circumstance that the duration of his life does not at all transgress the limits of probability as is the case with his predecessors."[5] Considering the fact that only from the time of Alexander's invasion on India fixing of precise dates in Indian history has been possible and also the inability of scholars to produce authentic evidence regarding the pre-Pārśva period, the historicity of Pārśva and Mahāvīra may be accepted.

Though no direct historical evidences are available even with regard to Pārśva we have some evidences. The Jaina inscriptions found in Mathura in Uttar Pradesh contain a dedicated reference to Ṛṣabha and some other Tīrthaṅkaras. Three important inscriptions may be cited here : (1) May the divine Ṛṣabha be pleased[6]; (2) Adoration to the Arhats[7]; (3) Adoration to the Arhat

of our age according to the Jaina tradition, were: Ajita, Sambhava, Abhinandana, Sumati, Padmaprabha, Supārśva, Candraprabha, Puṣpadanta or Suvidhi, Śītala, Śreyāṁsa, Vāsupūjya, Vimala, Ananta, Dharma, Śānti, Kunthu, Ara, Malli, Munisuvrata, Nimi, Nemi or Ariṣṭanemi and Pārśvanātha.

3 One *pūrva* year is considered to be equivalent to 70,560,000,000,000 years.

4 *Kalpa-Sūtra*, 227,182,168 & 147

5 *I.A.*, II, p. 261

6 *Epigraphica Indica*, I, 386, Inscr. VIII

7 *Ibid.*, I, 383, Inscr. III

Arhat Vardhamāna ![8] Commenting on the value of these inscriptions Cunningham writes: "The information derived from these inscriptions is of the greatest value for the ancient history of India. The general purport of all of them is the same—to record the gifts of certain individuals, for the honour of their religion; and for the benefit of themselves and their parents. When the inscriptions are confined to this simple announcement they are of little importance, but as the donors in most of these Mathura records have added the name of the reigning kings, and the saṁvat date at the time of the gift, they form in fact so many skeleton pages of the lost history . . ."[9] From our point of view these inscriptions indicate a very ancient origin of Jainism and also the probable succession of a number of Tīrthaṅkaras.

The *Kalpa-Sūtra*[10] and other Jaina works mention the fact that Pārśvanātha came to a hill in Patna before his 'release from bondage'. The hill is named 'Pāraśnāth Hill' and it seems to be a monumental evidence in regard to the historicity of Pārśva.

From a number of references to Pārśva and the Jainas in general in the Jaina classics we can maintain that the historicity of Pārśva at least cannot be denied and that Jainism was certainly older than Mahāvīra. We shall cite only a few passages here. The *Uttarādhyayana-Sūtra* records the meeting of Keśi (a follower of Pārśva) and Gautama (a disciple of Mahāvīra) and also the discussions they had regarding the differences between their two creeds.[11] The dispute is mentioned as having ended by the former accepting the latter's views.[12] We find the distinction between the four vows of the Pārśva school and the five vows of the Mahāvīra school.[13]

In some Hindu classics also we find references to the Jainas. The *Viṣṇu-Purāṇa*, the *Mahābhārata* and the *Manusmṛti* are cases in point. In our context the historical dates of the Hindu scriptures in which mention is made of Jainism is not important, for what impresses us (and the scholars in search of information regarding the antiquity of Jainism) is the fact that references are made to

[8] *Ibid*, I, 396, Inscr. VIII

[9] *Archaeological Survey of India Reports*, Vol. III, pp. 38-39

[10] 168

[11] XXIII. 9

[12] XXIII. 29

[13] XXIII. 12

the first Tīrthaṅkara, Ṛṣabha by name. Wilson, in his translation of the *Viṣṇu-Purāṇa* writes : "Nābhi had by his queen Maru the magnanimous Ṛṣabha, and he had a hundred sons, the eldest of whom was Bharata. Having ruled with equity and wisdom, and celebrated many sacrificial rites, he resigned the sovereignty of the earth to the heroic Bharata . . ."[14] In a foot-note on the *Bhāgavata-Purāṇa* Wilson adds : "That work enters much more into detail on the subject of Ṛṣabha's devotion, and particularizes circumstances not found in any other *Purāṇa*. The most interesting of these are the scenes of Ṛṣabha's wanderings which are said to be Konka, Venkata, Kutaka, and southern Karnataka, or the Western part of the Peninsula ; and the adoption of the Jaina belief by the people of those countries."[15] Emphasizing the historical value of the *Purāṇas* Bühler observes : "In particular must it be admitted that the persons introduced in the older, as well in the most recent, narratives are really historical characters. Although it is frequently the case that an individual is introduced at a period earlier or later than that to which he really belonged or that the most absurd stories are told with regard to him, yet there is no case forthcoming in which we could affirm with certainty that a man named by these chroniclers is a pure figment of the imagination. On the contrary, every freshly discovered inscription, every collection of old manuscripts, and every really historic work that is brought to light, furnishes confirmation of the actual existence of one or other of the characters described by them. In the same way all exact dates given by them deserve the most careful attention. When they are found to agree in two works of this class that are independent of one another they may, without hesitation, be accepted as historically correct."[16] The purport of all these in our context is that we have, in addition to the historical evidences, further evidences from the *Purāṇas* regarding the historicity of at least the last two Tīrthaṅkaras.

Among the modern scholars Colebrooke, Stevenson, Edward Thomas and Jarl Charpentier have held the opinion that Jainism is older than Mahāvīra. Charpentier observes : "We ought also to

[14] p. 163

[15] *Ibid.*, p. 164

[16] Uber da Leben des Jaina-Monches Hemacandra, p. 6 cited by C.J. Shah, *op. cit.*, pp. 191-192

remember both that the Jain religion is certainly older than Mahāvīra, his reputed predecessor, Pārśva, having almost certainly existed as the real person, and that consequently the main points of the original doctrine may have been codified long before Mahāvīra."[17] In a similar strain Dasgupta writes: "The story in the *Uttarādhyayana* that a disciple of Pārśva met a disciple of Mahāvīra and brought about the union of the old Jainism and that propounded by Mahāvīra seems to suggest that this Pārśva was probably a historical person."[18] From all these it is evident that Jainism was at least older than Mahāvīra.

[17] See Intr. to *Uttarādhyayana-Sūtra*, p. 21
[18] *op. cit.*, Vol. I, p. 169

3

Parsva and Mahavira

SINCE the historicity of Pārśva and Mahāvīra has been more or less authentically established it is interesting to inquire whether Mahāvīra modified the teachings of Pārśva in any respect. That Pārśva was the twenty-third Tīrthaṅkara and Mahāvīra, the twenty-fourth, has been conclusively proved by scholars but regarding the dates of Pārśva and Mahāvīra differences of opinion still persist. One view is that Pārśva was born about 872 B.C. and attained *nirvāṇa* around 772 B.C. and that Mahāvīra was born in 598 B.C. and died in 526 B.C. Another is that Pārśva was born in 817 B.C. and Mahāvīra, in 599 B.C.

The Jaina source-books contain distinct references to the differences between the teachings of Pārśva and Mahāvīra. The *Bhagavatī-Sūtra* draws the distinction between the four vows of Pārśva and the five vows of Mahāvīra. The reference is to a dispute between a follower of Pārśva and another of Mahāvīra. The passage concludes with the words that the former begged permission of the latter to stay with him "after having changed the law of the four vows for the five vows enjoining compulsory confession."[1]

Jacobi finds evidence for such a distinction in a Buddhist text *Sāmaññaphala Sutta*. Writing on the *sūtra*: *Catuyama Saṁvara samvuto* Jacobi maintains : "It is applied to the doctrine of Mahāvīra's predecessor, Pārśva, to distinguish it from the reformed creed of Mahāvīra, which is called *pañcayāma dharma*."[2] The five

[1] I. 76
[2] *I.A.*; IX, p. 160

yamas are the five great vows, *mahāvratāni* as they are usually named, viz., non-killing *(ahiṁsā)*, truthful speech *(sunrita)*, non-stealing *(asteya)*, celibacy (*brahmacarya*) and non-possession (*aparigraha*). In the *cāturyāma* of Pārśva *brahmacarya* was included in *aparigraha*.

The *Ācārāṅga* also makes a distinct reference to the *pañcayāma* of Mahāvīra.[3] We find references to the *cāturyāma* of Pārśva and *pañcayāma* of Mahāvīra in the *Uttarādhyayana* also.[4] The mention of the 'two forms' in the *Uttarādhyayana* is interpreted by Jacobi as follows: "The argumentation in the text presupposes a decay of the morals of the monastic order to have occurred between Pārśva and Mahāvīra, and this is possible only on the assumption of sufficient interval of time having elapsed between the last two Tīrthaṅkaras, and this perfectly agrees with the common tradition that Mahāvīra came 250 years after Pārśva."[5]

Though Jacobi's interpretation of the significance of the addition of celibacy to the list of vows finds general acceptance it is also held that Mahāvīra added the vow specifically because of the misbehaviour of one of his disciples, Gośāla. Gośāla, the founder of the *Ājīvika* sect of the Jainas did not keep to the faith and became unchaste and criticised the Jaina tradition even during the life-time of his master. According to some Mahāvīra added the vow of non-possession and not celibacy. They attribute Mahāvīra's going about the country unclothed to this addition. According to this school of thought Mahāvīra felt that the ascetic could free himself from all desires only when he got rid of all clothes, the fetters. Non-possession meant the giving up of home and kith and kin and having nothing even to sustain one's life. A third view that Mahāvīra insisted on celibacy as well as non-possession is also found. Umesha Mishra, for example writes : "Mahāvīra introduced the vow of celibacy even for the ascetics. Secondly he felt that the ascetics must completely conquer all their senses and emotions and become completely *nirlipta* in the world, and consequently cast off their clothes even. Mahāvīra probably felt that the ascetic could not be really free from good and evil as long as clothes fettered

[3] II, 15, 29

[4] XXIII. 23 & 16.

[5] See his trans. of *Uttarādhyayana*, f. n. for xxiii. 26

him."[6]

Though the differences are mentioned in the Jaina texts it is significant that the *Uttarādhyayana-Sūtra* maintains that in essence the teachings of Pārśva and Mahāvīra are the same. Kesi, one of Pārśva's followers is shown asking Sudharma-Gautama, one of Mahāvīra's disciples questions regarding the wisdom of the five vows. He asks : "Both Laws pursuing the same end, what has caused this difference ? Have you no misgivings about this two-fold law, O wise man ?"[7] Gautama replies : "Pārśvanātha understood the spirit of the time and realized that the enumeration of the great vows as four would suit people of his age; Mahāvīra gave the same four vows as five in order to make the Jaina doctrine more acceptable to the people of his time. There is no essential difference in the teachings of the two Tīrthaṅkaras."[8]

Sometimes the question of the exact vow included by Mahāvīra is discussed in the context of the Śvetāmbara-Digambara controversy regarding 'clothes'. One view is that Mahāvīra, as the reformer of the church preached against the ascetics being 'sky-clad' and the other[9] is that it was he who brought in the vow of non-possession and insisted on its logical extremes. But considering the fact that Mahāvīra permitted women to take to the ascetic vows whereas the Digambara sect maintained that *nirvāṇa* could not be attained by women and that they have to be born as men for realizing that state, the first of the views mentioned here seems to be more plausible. Also from the generally accepted view that there were no essential differences between the philosophical stand-points of the Śvetāmbaras and the Digambaras, in spite of a rigid division and in view of the fact that Mahāvīra is considered to have brought in certain changes in Pārśva's teachings, keeping in view, the 'changed circumstances' of his time it seems to be more appro-priate and correct to hold that Mahāvīra did not extend the law of

[6] *History of Indian Philosophy* (Allahabad : Tirabhukti Publications, 1957), Vol. I, p. 230

[7] XXIII. 24

[8] *Ibid.*, XXIII. 23-31

[9] U. Mishra, *op. cit.*, p. 230. It is interesting to note that even this scholar concedes that Mahāvīra emphasized the leading of an ethical life much more. "He believed that for the attainment of the highest truth it was most essential to purify one's body and mind through strict observance of the rules of good behav-iour." (*Ibid.*, p. 231)

non-possession to its absurd extreme. Since Mahāvīra is depicted as expressing great concern for the deterioration of morals in his own days we may conclude that the fifth vow added by him was in regard to *brahmacarya* and not in regard to *aparigraha*.

While concluding we may note down another important point of agreement between the two Tīrthaṅkaras, that on the constitution of the *Saṁgha*. They both agreed that monks and nuns as well as lay men and lay women could constitute the *Saṁgha*. But Mahāvīra distinguished between the ordinary lay man and the lay man who took to twelve vows. The two classes of lay men were respectively referred to as the *śrāvakas* and the *śramaṇopāsakas*. The *śrāvaka* had to merely express his faith in the principles of Jainism whereas the *śrāmaṇopāsaka* had to take five 'lesser vows' (*aṇuvratas*) and seven reinforcing vows (*śīlavratas*) which involved as self-imposition of 'boundaries' both in regard to the area of his wanderings and in regard to entertaining certain desires. Five 'great vows' (*mahāvratas*) were prescribed for the ascetics.

With all the differences referred to between the two philosophers we find the similarity between their ethical teachings shining forth and confirming the view that Mahāvīra was not a founder of a new sect but only continued with sincerity and devotion the tradition he inherited through a succession of Tīrthaṅkaras.

4

Svetambaras and Digambaras

Śvetāmbaras and Digambaras represent the two principal sects of the Jaina community. By and large the differences in regard to the general philosophy observable in the two sects are not of a fundamental character. This is evident from the fact that both the sects consider a Jaina classic *Tattvārthādhigama-Sūtra* as most authoritative. The author of the work was probably a Śvetāmbara, but the Digambaras also regard it as one of their primary source-books. All the same for a non-Jaina the puritan spirit of the Digambaras is so striking that he thinks that there are fundamental differences between thc Śvetāmbaras and the Digambaras. That the differences are negligible will become clear from the sequel but it is interesting to note what a Śvetāmbara is reported to have said: "We are the catholics amongst the Jains; the Digambaras represent the puritan."[1] This explains the extremism, at least in regard to the outward appearance, of the Digambaras.

The Digambaras went about 'clothed in space', (the term *dik* stands here for space and *aṁbara*, for clothes) impressing upon the world that they belonged to no group or community but to the whole of humanity and proclaiming that they had got over the last determining marks by casting off their clothes.

Zimmer's remarks on religion in general offers us an insight into the motivations responsible for the Digambaras insisting on becoming complete 'non-entities'. He writes: "Religion is supposed

[1] See *Encyclopaedia of Religion & Ethics*, Vol. 22, p. 123

finally to release us from the desires and fears, ambitions and commitments of secular life, . . . for religion claims the soul . . . But then religion is a community affair and so itself is an instrument of bondage . . . Anyone seeking to transcend the tight complacencies of his community must break away from the religious congregation. One of the classic ways of doing this is by becoming a monk . . . dedicated to isolation from, and insurance against, the ordinary human bondages."[2]

The Digambaras were, at the time of Alexander's invasion of India (327-326 B.C.) a sizable group and the Greek historians refer to them as *gymnosophists*, the naked philosophers. The Digambara cult continued probably till 1000 A.D. when the Muslim rulers prohibited 'nudity'.

The Śvetāmbaras were the 'white-clad' (the term *śveta* means white) and the white garment signified their ideal of purity; the catholic outlook of the sect is apparent. Not making any great departure from the spirit of Jainism they exhibited serious concern for decency. One version is that Mahāvīra tried to bring about this healthy change in the adherents of the Jaina faith as also the admission of women into the 'Order' (*Saṁgha*). Some scholars however hold that Mahāvīra was a 'gymnosophist'. If this view were correct it would be difficult for us to account for the reforms he is said to have brought into the Jaina church, for, one of the strongest beliefs of the Digambaras is that women should not be admitted into the *Saṁgha* and Mahāvīra pleaded for their admission.

It seems certain that even at the time of Mahāvīra the two sects were in existence, though he was able to maintain at least a semblance of unity between them. The final 'parting of ways' came much later. Some scholars like Zimmer have discussed the question whether, in point of time, the one or the other sect came first. But it seems to be more fruitful to analyse how and when the split came, for, both the sects are recognised as reflecting the spirit of Jainism. Very likely, therefore, the Jaina community was affected by the divisive forces inherent in the nature of any social institution. We find various versions in regard to the schisms.

2 *Philosophies of India* (London : Routledge & Kegan Paul, 1953), pp. 158–159

The Śvetāmbara version identifies two factors which might have effected the division. The first was a 12-year famine that swept Magadha during Chandragupta's period (around 310 B.C.). To escape from the famine twelve thousand monks, under the leadership of Bhadrabāhu, went down to the south but were strictly adhering to the rule of nudity. During his absence, Sthūlabhadra officiated as the chief in the north and he relaxed the rule and he allowed the monks from both the sects to wear clothes. After Bhadrabāhu's return he became the leader again though he could not, any longer, insist on even some of the monks being clad in space. Bhadrabāhu was not very happy. Secondly, during Bhadrabāhu's absence from Magadha, Sthūlabhadra called a council at Pāṭalīputra to collect and edit the sacred books. The council could produce only eleven *Aṅgas* and the twelfth *Aṅga*, which contained the fourteen *Pūrvas* could not be produced. Since Sthūlabhadra knew the fourteen *Pūrvas* well he supplied them and the twelfth *Aṅga* was 'recast.' Bharabāhu didn't like this development either; he was annoyed at the council having met during his absence and refused to recognize the twelfth *Aṅga* as well as the other *Aṅgas* recast by the council. The division became permanent only in 83 A.D. (142 A.D. according to another view). The Digambaras maintain that it was Bhadrabāhu, the eighth successor to Mahāvīra who was responsible for the laxer principles and this was the Śvetāmbara sect which came to be formed in 80 A.D. We find an interesting legend to pinpoint the occasion which necessitated the two-fold division : A monk named Śivabhūti had been given a beautiful blanket by the King in whose service he had been at the time of his initiation. His spiritual preceptor warned him that it was becoming a snare to him and advised him to give it away; this he refused to do, so his preceptor took the extreme step of tearing up the blanket in its owner's absence. Śivabhūti, when he discovered what had happened, was so angry that he declared that, if he could not have that one possession which he valued, he would keep nothing at all, but would wander in entire nakedness . . . and then and there he started a new sect, that of the naked Digambaras.[3]

Related to the story narrated above is the attempt of Śivabhūti's sister wanting to join the *Saṁgha* and being denied admission.

[3] See *Encyclopaedia of Religion & Ethics*, Vol. 12, p. 123

Seeing that it was impracticable for a woman to go about nude, Śivabhūti told his sister that it was impossible for a woman to become a nun, or to obtain release without rebirth as a man. Though the legend itself may or may not reflect a historical fact, the fact that the Digambaras strictly prohibited women joining the order gives some plausibility to the legend itself, especially Śivabhūti's refusing consent to his sister becoming a nun.

We shall note down some points of distinction between the two sects:

In regard to the Tīrthaṅkaras:

The symbols given by the two sects to the idols differ.

The Śvetāmbara tradition depicts the idols as wearing a loincloth, bedecked with jewels and with glass eyes inserted in the marble.

The Digambara tradition represents the Tīrthaṅkaras as nude and with down-cast eyes.

In regard to Mahāvīra:

The Śvetāmbaras believe that Mahāvīra was born of a *kṣatriya* lady, Triśāla though conception took place in the womb of a *brāhmaṇa* lady, Devānanda. The change of embryo is believed to have been effected by God Indra on the eighty-third day after conception. We find references to the legend in at least three Jaina source-books, viz., the *Ācārāṅga*, *Kalpa-Sūtra* and the *Bhagavatī-Sūtra*. It is quite likely, the story was invented by the author of the *Kalpa-Sūtra* as an occasion to express the prevailing sentiment of contempt of the *brāhmaṇas* and that it was later on embodied in the *Ācārāṅga*. Jacobi's interpretation of the episode is that Siddhārtha (Mahāvīra's father) had two wives, one a *brāhmaṇa* lady, Devānanda, and another a *kṣatriya* lady, Triśāla and that to enable the offspring opportunities of being patronised it was considered to be that of the *kṣatriya* lady. But when we remember that in those days inter-caste marriages were looked down upon, Jacobi's interpretation is not quite acceptable. May be, Devānanda was a foster-mother and not the real mother. The scriptural support for this is the *Ācārāṅga* which refers to the five nurses who attended on the child Mahāvīra, and one of them was a wet-nurse. The Digambaras dismiss the whole episode as unreliable and absurd.

The Śvetāmbara biographies picture Mahāvīra to have been extremely philosophical from his childhood days; though he wanted to renounce the world in his early years, in deference to his parents' wishes he did not do so. The Digambara version is that by his thirtieth year Mahāvīra suddenly renounced the world being disgusted with the ephimeral nature of things and that till then he, like any other prince, enjoyed all the luxuries of a palace life.

The Śvetāmbaras have recorded that Mahāvīra was married at a fairly young age and that he led a full-fledged house-holder's life till he was thirty, when, he became an ascetic. This version is in keeping with the Śvetāmbara belief that Mahāvīra's parents were highly alarmed at the child's unusual reflective bent of mind and sense of renunciation and wanted to divert his attention by marrying him off early and providing him with an atmosphere of worldly joy and pleasure. Mahāvīra is depicted as having married princess Yaśoda.

The Digambaras deny the fact of marriage altogether. They quote verses from the *Paumacariya* and *Āvaśyaka Niryukti* which contain details about the lives of various Tīrthaṅkaras. A contrast is made in these books between the 12th, 19th, 22nd, 23rd and 24th Tīrthaṅkara (Mahāvīra) on the one hand and all the rest of the Tīrthaṅkaras on the other. Whereas the five Tīrthaṅkaras mentioned here renounced the world when they were still *kumāras* the others did so after having ruled over their respective states. It should be noted here that the term *kumāra* is used in two senses in Saṁskrit: to denote a prince and also a celibate. From the context in which the term is used in the books referred to, it seems certain that Mahāvīra is not referred to as *kumāra* in the sense of his being a celibate. It might have happened, of course, that he married much against his own wishes but that he married seems to be fairly well-established.

The Śvetāmbaras hold that though Mahāvīra was keen on renouncing the world earlier, he promised his mother that during his parents' life-time he would not become an ascetic. The promise was in response to the persuasions of his mother. Even after his parents' death, Mahāvīra took his elder brother's permission and then only renounced the world. All this, the Śvetāmbaras claim, signify their teacher's taking care not to hurt anybody before his initiation. The Digambaras maintain that even during his parents' life-time and much against their wishes Mahāvīra took to renunciation.

In regard to source-books :

The Śvetāmbaras maintain that the fourteen *Pūrvas* were lost and that the first eleven *Aṅgas* are not extinct. The Digambaras believe that the *Pūrvas* as well as the *Aṅgas* were lost. They refused to accept the achievements of the first Council which met under the leadership of Sthūlabhadra and, consequently the recasting of the *Aṅgas.*

The lists of non-canonical works of the two sects differ considerably.

The Śvetāmbaras did not allow laymen to read their scriptures, whereas the Digambaras permitted even the common man to have access to the sacred scriptures.

In regard to women :

The Śvetāmbaras believed that a woman could become a Tīrthaṅkara and so they allowed women into the ascetic order. The Digambaras did not allow women to join the *Saṁgha* and maintained that women could attain the Tīrthaṅkara-status only after being born as men.

In regard to sub-divisions :

The Śvetāmbaras were divided into the non-idol-worshipping (*sthānakavāsi*) and the idol-worshipping (*deravāsi*) groups. There were four main sub-divisions among the Digambaras : the *kāsṭhāsaṁgha, mūlasaṁgha, mathurasaṁgha* and *gopyasaṁgha.* There were only minor differences. The fourth sub-division agreed with the Śvetāmbaras in most respects.

In regard to ascetics :

The Śvetāmbara ascetic is allowed to have fourteen possessions including his loin-cloth, shoulder-cloth, etc. He was allowed to move from place to place and it is not surprising that the laymen complain that sometimes there is too much of interference from the ascetics. The Digambara ascetic is allowed to have only two possessions, a peacock's feather and a brush and has to live entirely in the jungle.

In regard to biographies of great teachers :

The Śvetāmbaras use the term *Caritra* and the Digambaras make use of the term *Purāṇa*.

5

Jaina Source-books

SINCE Jainism itself was older than Mahāvīra it is evident that not all canonical works are attributable to the twenty-fourth Tīrthaṅkara. Certainly the discourses delivered by him are considered to be extremely significant and find a place in the canons and reflect the Jaina tradition in all its essential aspects.

Our difficulty in understanding Jainism stems as much from its antiquity as from the absence of written records of the philosophical ideas of the long line of teachers till the 5th Century A.D. when probably redaction of the canons took place. Since different dates have been given to the Councils which set about the task of 'fixing the canons' our attempt to study the history of Jainism is beset with difficulties. Also, in regard to the achievements of the Councils themselves opinions differ. According to one version the first Council met at Pāṭalīputra (by about 300 B.C.) and only ten of the fourteen *Pūrvas* were 'recast' but the achievements were not accepted by a section of the Jains. Thus according to this view the origin of the *Siddhānta* is identified with the recasting of the ten *Pūrvas* and other *Aṅgas*.

Jarl Charpentier, rejecting the thesis that only ten *Pūrvas* were redacted in the first Council and by implication also the thesis that at the time of the Council none of the fourteen Pūrvas was in existence, writes: "...not only the fourth *Aṅga* but also the *Nandi-Sūtra*, a scripture of certainly more recent date, actually knew all the fourteen *Pūrvas*; and those were all incorporated in the *Dṛṣṭivāda*, the twelfth *Aṅga*, of which we have reports from a still later date.

Moreover, the commentaries on the *Aṅgas* and other canonical scriptures contain, in some passages, quotations from the *Pūrvas*. And this shows, no doubt, that they were in existence at a time much later than that of the Council held in 300 B.C. This fact implies...that the old scriptures really existed even after the time of Bhadrabāhu and Sthūlabhadra."[1]

Till then the teachings were transmitted through oral tradition merely. During the process of oral transmission itself many changes in the teachings might have been introduced with the result that even the first composition of the works cannot be considered authentic. There is reason to believe that before the final edition of the works many additions and alterations as also transposition of parts of the compositions took place. The fact that first a language Ardha-Māgadhī was used and later Māgadhī was employed add to the complexity of the problem of disentangling the various strands of Jaina thought.

The works as we find them today as the source-books reflect the varied styles and methods of presentation adopted by the teachers and their commentators. While we find some books in pure prose we do not find the poetic presentation of abstract philosophical doctrines being completely absent in some works. The combination of prose and poetry is not infrequently met with while vague and repetitious exposition characterize some canonical works. Beyond all the thick sheaths we do find the kernel of a systematic and logically argued-out philosophical position which can compare favourably with other highly developed Indian as well as Western philosophical movements.

The source-books of the Jainas are classified under seven different heads. We shall consider them in order.

I The Pūrvas :

The *Pūrvas*, fourteen in number, are considered to constitute the oldest part of the Jaina canon. According to one view the *Pūrvas* are traceable to the first Tīrthaṅkara, Ṛṣabha. According to another the *Pūrvas* were taught by Mahāvīra himself while

[1] *Uttarādhyayana-Sūtra* (Uppsala : Appelbergs Boktryckeri Aktiebo lag, 1922), Intr., p. 15

his apostles (*gaṇadharas*) composed the *Aṅgas*. Jacobi relies on the second version and Charpentier also contributes to the view. except that he doubts "whether the statement concerning the connection between the *gaṇadharas* and the *Aṅgas* can be of much value, as there are eleven of them both, i.e., eleven *gaṇadharas* and eleven *Aṅgas*[2], after the loss of the twelfth *Aṅga*."[3] This coincidence according to him suggests that "the whole story may have been invented at a later date."[4]

The traditional belief among the Śvetāmbaras and Digambaras is that the *Pūrvas* have been completely and irrecoverably lost. In *Aṅga* 4 and in the *Nandi-Sūtra* we find a table of contents, and, according to this the fourteen *Pūrvas* were : *Utpāda*, *Agrāyaṇīya*, *Vīryapravāda*, *Astināstipravāda*, *Jñānapravāda*, *Satyapravāda*, *Ātmapravāda*, *Karmapravāda*, *Pratyākhyānapravāda*, *Vidyānupravāda*, *Avandhya*, *Prāṇāyuh*, *Kriyāviśala* and *Lokabindusāra*.

II The Aṅgas :

The *Aṅga* literature constitutes the oldest source-material on Jainism available. We shall dwell at some length on the twelve *Aṅgas*.

Ācārāṅga : This is the oldest of the *Aṅgas* and it contains two books called the *śrutaskandhas*. They differ very much in style and the way in which their respective subject-matters are treated. Probably the first of the *śrutaskandhas* is responsible for the opinion that the *Ācārāṅga* represents the ancient part of the *Siddhānta*.

We find prose passages as well as poetic descriptions. They both treat of the mode of life (*ācāra*) of the Jaina clergy. These are believed to be the records of Mahāvīra's teachings to one of his disciples, Sudharman, who in turn transmitted them orally to his disciple Jambu.

The prose passages commence with the words : "I have heard, O long-lived one ! Thus has that saint spoken." Here 'I' stands for Sudharman and 'that saint' for Mahāvīra. Long passages have, as their concluding sentence "Thus I say".

[2] Italics mine.
[3] *op. cit.*, pp. 11-12
[4] *Ibid.*, p. 12

We find general references to the teachings, as for example : "The Arhats...of the past, present and future, all say thus, speak thus, declare thus, explain thus; all breathing, existing, living, sentience, be not abused, not tormented, and not driven away."

We also find sermons embodying the stern tradition. For instance we find a passage like this : "This is the pure, unchallengeable, eternal law, which the clever ones, who understand the world have declared. Having adopted the law, one should not hide it, nor forsake it. Correctly understanding the law, one should arrive at indifference for the impressions of the senses, and not act on the motives of the world....Those who acquiesce and indulge (in worldly pleasures) are born again and again ... if careful, thou wilt conquer. Thus I say."

Sūtrakṛtāṅga : This book also is divided into two parts and the first of these, like the first *śrutaskandha* of the *Ācārāṅga* is considered by eminent Jaina scholars to belong to the older part of the Jaina canon. It is significant that this *Aṅga* contains arguments against *Kriyavāda*, *Akriyavāda*, *Vaināyika* and *Ajñānavāda*.

This *Aṅga*, like the previous one is a synthesis of prose and poetry and has a number of parables which do remind us of the parables of Buddhism. The main subject-matter of this *Aṅga* is the expression of concern for the young men who have been initiated into Jainism. The young monks are warned of the temptations that the heretic doctrines might offer them. We find the following passage : "As birds of prey ... carry off a fluttering bird whose wings are not yet grown ... so many unprincipled men will seduce a novice who has not yet mastered the Law."

One of the heretical schools referred to is that of the Buddhists, and their doctrines are refuted. With all this, as Winternitz points out, the view of life (*saṁsāra*) that we find in the *Ācārāṅga* is not substantially different from what we find in Buddhism. For example, we find the words : "It is not myself alone who suffers, all creatures in the world suffer; this a wise man should consider, and he should patiently bear (such calamities) as befall him, without giving way to his passion."

Sthānāṅga & *Samavāyāṅga* : They embody an encyclopaedic knowledge of the Jaina philosophy and an historical account of the Jaina teachers. In the first one we have a table of contents of the twelfth *Aṅga*, the *Dṛṣṭivāda*, and it contains specific references to the seven schisms. The latter *Aṅga* incorporates in itself some extracts from all the twelve *Aṅgas*.

Bhagavatī : This is considered to be a very sacred source-book since it deals with the contemporaries of Mahāvīra and those who came before him. The book treats of the rival schools founded by Gośāla and Jamāli. Weber's conclusion that Jainism is of a very ancient origin is based on this text.

Jñātādharmakathāḥ : The main characteristic of this book is that it is narrative in content and contains a number of parables from each one of which a moral is drawn and proclaimed. Weber points out : "All these legends give us the impression of containing traditions which have been handed down in good faith. They offer, in all probability (especially as they frequently agree with the Buddhist legends) most important evidence for the period of the life of Mahāvīra himself."[5]

A serious student of Indian thought cannot but be reminded here of the *Purāṇa* literature of the Hindus and *Jātaka* literature of the Buddhists. The narrations are aimed at conveying highly significant moral principles in the form of extremely simple stories and interesting parables. For instance, the first book of this *Aṅga* contains the story of a merchant having four daughters-in-law. Wanting to 'test' them, he gives each one five grains of rice, with the specific instruction that they should give them back to him when he asks for the same. The first daughter-in-law, with indifference throws the grains away with the thought that when the father-in-law asks for the grains, she could easily take some from the godown. The second one eats the grains. The third carefully preserves the grains and the fourth one sows them and when the merchant asks for the grains she has a lot of stock.[6] The aim of the parable is to classify monks into four types : the monks who are not at all serious about the five vows, the monks who neglect the vows, the monks who adhere to the vows scrupulously and strictly and lastly the monks who not only adhere to the vows but also propagate them.

Upāsakadaśāḥ, *Antakṛddaśāḥ* & *Anuttaraupapādikadaśāh* : These are all narrative in content and contain a number of parables

[5] *I. A.*, XIX, p. 65
[6] *Jñatā-Sūtra*, 63

to exhort men to adopt the ascetic way of life. The point is brought home to the minds of the people by suggesting that even laymen who renounce their riches get miraculous powers and die as saints to get the exalted status of gods.

The *Upāsakadaśāḥ* is an exposition, in ten chapters, of the religious duties of an *Upāsaka*.[7] Every chapter has a story, about the pious *śrāvakas*.[8] The first story is especially significant in our context. It describes the visit of Mahāvīra to a small suburb called Kollaga, outside the city of Vaniyagama[9] and Ānanda's paying obesience to Mahāvīra[10] and listening to Mahāvīra's exposition of the Law.[11] He expresses faith in the doctrine but says : " ... Still though acknowledging this, many kings, princes, nobles, governors, mayors, bankers, merchants and others have, in your presence, ... renounced the life of a house-holder, and entered the monastic state. But I will, in your presence, ... take on myself the twelve-fold law of the house-holder, which consists of the five lesser vows and the seven disciplinary vows ... May it ... please you ... Do not deny me !"[12]

The other legends also are about rich men, who, even without formally renouncing the world but by adopting the *ascetic attitude* are rewarded with remarkable powers which enable them to be born as gods in the heavens.[13] To those critics who assail Jainism for its extreme asceticism, the parable offers an answer in that it emphasizes not asceticism but the ascetic temperament, not formally becoming a saint but becoming truly saintly. Many misunderstandings about Jainism are traceable to the view that Jainism has gone to the extremes in regard to asceticism and non-violence. Since the insistence on the spirit of renunciation is found in one of the ancient source-books of Jainism, the charge that referring to the spirit of, rather than the actual entrance into, asceticism is the

7 In Jainism the term stands for a person who has accepted the teachings of Mahāvīra, without renouncing the world and adopting the ascetic vows. The taking of the lesser vows is not inconsistent with life in society and so the *upāsaka* continues to be a house-holder.

8 *Upāsakadaśāḥ* : i, 2

9 *Ibid.*, i, 7 & 9

10 *Ibid.*, i, 10

11 *Ibid.*, i, 11

12 *Ibid.*, i, 12

13 *Ibid.*, i, 63

interpretation of modern scholars cannot be held. Our opinion that Jainism has not gone to the extremes in regard to renunciation gets confirmed when we find, in the eighth and ninth *Aṅgas*, legends similar to those found in the seventh exhorting people to lead a pious and non-attached worldly life.[14]

Praśnavyākaraṇāni : This deals first with the five evils to be avoided—injury to life, lying, robbery, unchastity, love and possession and then treats of the five positive virtues.[15]

Vipākaśrutas : This *Aṅga* is full of legends illustrating the effects of good and evil deeds.

Dṛṣṭivāda : This is no longer extant. This *Aṅga* is believed to have incorporated all the fourteen *Pūrvas*. Eminent scholars of Europe are of the opinion that no convincing reasons are adduced by the Jainas themselves for the loss of the twelfth *Aṅga*. Weber maintains that the Jainas have wantonly rejected it since they found no accord between the orthodox tradition and the teachings of the *Dṛṣṭivāda*.[16] Jacobi's view is that since the *Aṅga* incorporated merely the philosophical discussions between Mahāvīra and his rivals, it would have become completely unintelligible or at least lost all interest to the Jainas themselves.[17] Leumann feels that the text must have dealt with astrology, sorcery, etc. and, as such, must have been allowed to have become obsolete.[18] The general view of the three scholars seems to be that the Jainas themselves disregarded the twelfth *Aṅga* but this may not really be the case since the Jainas themselves say that the *Pūrvas* became lost only gradually.

III Upāṅgas :

Though the number of *Upāṅgas* corresponds to that of the *Aṅgas* (for they are also considered to be twelve in number), even a cursory glance of the *Upāṅgas* lays bare the fact that there is no inner connection between the *Aṅgas* and the *Upāṅgas*.

Aupapādika : This *Upāṅga* is historically significant. It describes in detail the meeting between King Ajātasatru and Mahāvīra

14 See Barnett, *Antakṛddaśāḥ* & *Anuttaraupapādikadaśāḥ*, pp. 15, 16 & 110.
15 *I.A.*, XX, p. 23
16 *I.A.*, XVII, p. 286
17 *Jaina Sūtras*, pt. I, Intr., p. xlv ff
18 Cited by C.J. Shah. *op. cit.*, p. 231 f. n.

and the sermons he gave regarding reincarnation and salvation.

Rājapraśnīya : As the title itself suggests, the quientessence of the *Upāṅga* consists in the questions addressed by a King (King Paesi) to a saint (Keśi) regarding the relation between soul and body. The King, at the end of the 'session' accepts Jainism.

Jivābhigama and Prajñāpana : These two *Upāṅgas* deal with animate and inanimate aspects of nature.

Sūryaprajñāpti, Jaṁbūdvīpaprajñāpti & Candraprajñāpti : These three deal respectively with Indian astronomy, geography of India and cosmography of the heavens.

Niryāvalī, Kalpāvataṁsikāḥ, Puṣpikāḥ, Puṣpacūlikāḥ & Vṛṣṇida-saḥ : These five probably form parts of a single text *Niryāvalī-Sūtra*. The enumeration of the five might have been caused by the desire to have twelve *Upāṅgas*.

IV *Prakīrṇas* :

These are ten in number and as the name itself denotes they are scattered and hastily sketched pieces. In these many different subjects are treated. The ten *Prakīrṇas* are : *Catuḥśaraṇa, Āturapra-tyākhyāna, Bhaktaparijñā, Samstāra, Taṇḍulavaitālīka, Candravedhy-aka, Devendrastava, Gaṇitavidyā, Mahapratyākhyāna* and *Vīrasatva.*

V *Cheda-Sūtras* :

These are six in number and deal with prohibited conduct for monks and nuns prescribing punishments and expiations for the same. These correspond roughly to the *Vinaya* texts of the Buddhists. *Niśītha, Mahāniśītha, Vyavahāra, Ācāradaśāḥ Bṛhatkalpa* and *Pañcakalpa* are the *Cheda-Sūtras.*

VI *Mūla-Sūtras* :

As the name itself indicates they are the 'original' texts. They denote the recorded works of Lord Mahāvīra himself. As such these *Sūtras* are important. These are four in number.

Uttarādhyayana-Sūtra : This is similar in content to the *Sūtra-kṛtāṅga.* References to the heretical doctrines are infrequent.

Āvaśyaka-Sūtra : This deals in detail with the six observances obligatory on all Jainas, be they laymen or clergymen.

Daśavaikālika : This deals with the rules of conduct of the Jaina clergy.

Piṇḍaniryukti : This is just a supplement to the previous *Sūtra.*

VII Two Solitary Texts : *Nandi-Sūtra & Anuyogadvāra-Sūtra* :

These contain encyclopaedic information regarding the source-books and regarding the proper modes of interpreting the sacred texts.

6

Is Jainism Atheistic?

ACCORDING to the two-fold division of systems of Indian philosophy, — into the orthodox (*āstika*) and the heterodox (*nāstika*), — Jainism, along with the Cārvāka and the Buddhist systems is grouped under the heterodox systems.

Of the three senses in which the term *nāstika* is made use of in the Indian tradition, viz., disbelief in a life beyond, disbelief in the authority of the Veda and disbelief in God — Jainism cannot be classified as a *nāstika* system in the first sense since it does not maintain that death is the end of life, that after death nothing exists. Belief in the doctrine of *karma* and the doctrine of transmigration of souls which are considered foundational to the edifice of the classical six systems of Indian philosophy are the accepted fundamental tenets in Jainism as well. The description of the four states of being (*jīva*) clearly indicates that Jainism was not a crude *nāstika* system. The exhortation found in Jainism for man to live an ethical life so that he won't slip down the scale of spiritual evolution together with the insistence on aiming at complete freedom from the shackles of matter (*karma*) clear the misunderstanding that Jaina heterodoxy is analogous to that of the Cārvākas.

In regard to the second interpretation, there can be no two opinions on the fact that Jainism is clearly anti-Vedic. Jainism does not accept the authenticity and authoritativeness of the Vedic teaching but this in itself was not due to disbelief in speculative and metaphysical analyses of the human situation. The Jaina psychology, metaphysics and epistemology are positive evidences to the fact that rejection of Vedic authority was not necessitated by an aversion to philosophical speculation. The Jaina tradition had its own line of teachers and sages and also sacred books containing philosophic wisdom. These 'books' were considered authoritative by the Jainas. The Jainas believe that their scriptures give right knowledge since they embody the utterances of persons who had themselves lived a worldly life but who perfected themselves by means of right actions and right knowledge.

The third interpretation of *nāstika* as one who does not believe in God is extremely important, since the popular understanding of the term invariably equates it with the term *atheism*. To categorically dub Jainism as atheistic is both unwarranted and unphilosophical, for we find in Jainism only the rejection of a 'supremely personal god' and not godhead itself.

R. Garbe makes a significant distinction between naive and philosophical atheism. He points out that naive atheism is to be traced to the Vedic age. "In the *Ṛg Veda* the national god, Indra is denied in several passages;[1] and we read of people who absolutely denied his existence[2] even in those early days. We have here the first traces of that naive atheism which is so far from indulging in any philosophical reflection that it simply refuses to believe what it cannot visualize, and which, in a later period, was known as the disbelief of the Lokāyata system; that is to say, of crass materialism. It is different with the atheism which had grown into a conviction as a result of serious philosophical speculation; this, in distinction from the other naive form, we may describe briefly as *philosophic* atheism."[3]

Jaina atheism, if properly interpreted, belongs to the category of philosophic atheism, for there is a deep analysis of the concept of God as the Supreme Cause of the Universe and a systematic refutation of the arguments of the philosophers, who have sought to prove the existence of God. The term god is used in Jainism to denote a higher state of existence of the *jīva* or the conscious principle. The system believes that this state of godly existence is only a shade better than that of the ordinary human being, for, it is not

[1] IV. 24. 10; X. 119
[2] II. 12. 5; VIII. 100. 3
[3] *Encyclopaedia of Religion & Ethics*, Vol. 11, p. 185

free from the cycle of birth and death. The longest period of celestial existence in the highest heaven *Sarvārthasiddhi* is between 32 and 33 'oceans of years' (*sāgaropamas*). The moment the 'gods' exhaust their good *karmas* because of which they attained a better status than that of the ordinary human beings, they have to come down to the earth, unless, in the meanwhile they gain the saving knowledge which enables them to come out of the vicious circle of birth and death.

The liberated souls, according to the Jaina view, go up the top of the universe and they are those who have perfected themselves absolutely and hence are those who have no longer to 'face the fall,' for they eternally remain there. They have cut themselves away from the world of life and death (*saṁsāra*) and so, by hypothesis cannot exert any influence over it. Hence the functions of a Supreme Ruler, Creator and Regulator cannot be attributed to them. In regard to others who are still in *saṁsāra* they cannot be regarded as eternal gods. It is in this sense that the Tīrthaṅkara's is a more covetable position than that of 'god.' Attaining the status of the Tīrthaṅkara is the aim of life and the Tīrthaṅkara is the shining example to humanity, assuring it that spiritual perfection is attainable and is not merely a speculative value.

In understanding the atheistic aspects of Jaina philosophy one other remark of Garbe regarding the gods in India is helpful. He says: "In India, recognition of these faded gods of the people has been fully reconciled with the atheistic view of the world. In the Sāṁkhya system, belief in gods who have risen to evanescent godhead (*janyeśvara*, *kāryeśvara*) has nothing whatever to do with the question of God Eternal (*nityeśvara*), as regards whom the theists assume that He made the world with His will. The use of a special term (*Īśvara*, the powerful) in Indian philosophy obviously arose out of the endeavour to distinguish this God even verbally from the shadow-like gods of the people (*deva*)."[4]

In this connection it is well to remember that even some of the orthodox systems — among the six classical ones — have been repudiating belief in God. The Nyāya and Vaiśeṣika systems for example were originally atheistic and became theistic only after their fusion. The Sāṁkhya system similarly denied the existence of

[4] *Ibid.*, p. 185

God. In fact this was one of the characteristic features of the Sāṁkhya system and the system itself is referred to as 'god-less' (*nirīśvara*). Many of the *sūtras* maintain that God's existence cannot be proved.[5] The Bhātta school of the Mīmāṁsakas similarly denies the existence of a Supreme God.[6]

Let us now consider the Jaina repudiation of God's existence. Jainism, unlike the theistic schools does *not* accept the existence of a supreme creator and sustainer of the world. The system maintains that the world is without a beginning and an end. In this we see the most consistent theory of realism, it being maintained that each and every one of the categories is eternally real and hence that logically they are in no need of postulating a god who is the supreme cause and ruler of the world. Acārya Jīnasena asks : "If God created the universe, where was he before creating it ? If he was not in space, where did he localise the universe ? How could a formless or immaterial substance like God create the world of matter ? If the material is to be taken as existing, why not take the world itself as unbegun ? If the creator was uncreated, why not suppose the world to be itself self-existing ?" Then he continues : "Is God self-sufficient ? If he is, he need not have created the world. If he is not, like an ordinary potter, he would be incapable of the task, since, by hypothesis, only a perfect being could produce it......"[7]

The Jaina philosopher pertinently asks : "If every existent object must have a maker, that maker himself would be explained by another — his maker, etc. To escape from this vicious circle we have to assume that there is one uncreated, self-explaining cause, god. But then, if it is maintained that one being can be self-subsistent, why not say that there are many others also who are uncreated and eternal similarly ?" Hence "it is not necessary to assume the existence of any first cause of the universe."[8] S. Radhakrishnan states the Jaina point of view thus : "The Jaina view is that the whole universe of being, of mental and material factors has existed from all eternity, undergoing an infinite number of revolutions produced by the powers of nature without the intervention of any external deity. The diversities of the world are traced to the five

[5] I, 92-94; V. 2-12; 46, 126 & 127; VI. 64 & 65

[6] Sec 16

[7] *Ādi Purāṇa*, Chap. III (Cited in C.J. Shah, *op. cit.*, p. 35)

[8] Hemacandra, *Syādvādamañjarī*, Verse 6

co-operating conditions of time (*kāla*), nature (*svabhāva*), necessity (*niyati*), activity (*karma*) and desire to be and act (*udyama*)."[9]

The Jainas' view of god is thus conditioned by their conviction that the world is uncreated and indestructible. Since the theists postulate the existence of god to account for the world of name, form and experiences, the Jainas are critical of every one of the arguments brought forth by the theists. Since the Jaina philosophers were most vigorous in rebutting the Nyāya philosopher's arguments,[10] we shall refer to them alone here.

One of the arguments of the Nyāya philosopher is that the world as an effect implies a cause, an intelligent cause and that is god. The Jaina philosopher maintains that if on the analogy of ordinary effects having intelligent human causes it is argued that the world has god as its cause, it should also be held that like man, god is also imperfect. If, on the other hand, it is said that the similarity between the two types of causation is not so striking, the Jaina philosopher maintains, the Nyāya philosopher is also not justified in drawing the inference he does. Because water-vapour is similar to smoke, there can be no justification in inferring fire from water-vapour as from smoke. The third alternative, — of maintaining that the world as effect is different from other effects (and so justifying a different type of cause) — is again not accepted by the Jaina philosopher. He maintains that the most important thing about a cause regarding the world-creation and an ordinary effect like a house getting gradually ruined is that the cause is invisible and so it should be accepted also that the ruins too were produced by intelligent agents.

Proceeding on the analogy of the ordinary creator — the causal agent for a given effect — the Jaina philosopher argues that god as the causal agent for the world must also be considered to have a body. We have never seen any intelligent creator without a body and so the case cannot be different with the creator of the world, argues the Jaina philosopher.

The Jaina philosopher analyses the various other possibilities also — even if a bodiless god is admitted to exist and is considered responsible for creation. Creation may be due to his personal whim

9 *Indian Philosophy*, p. 330

10 See *Syādvādamañjarī* & *Ṣaḍdarśanasamuccaya*

or due to good and bad actions of men or due to god's mercy on men or due to god considering creation itself to be a play. The Jaina philosopher points out that none of the four alternatives gives us a creditable account of god as a perfect being far removed from humanity in the matter of his various endowments. Admitting god to have created the world out of his personal whim would do away with all natural laws governing the world. If good and bad actions are responsible for world-creation, god's independence would suffer, for he will then not be responsible for the good and bad experiences of men. Pointing out that out of mercy on humanity god created the world is still not a satisfactory argument since this can't account for the presence of suffering in the world. If, in this context, good and bad acts respectively are held responsible for enjoyment and suffering, god becomes a superfluous entity. The last alternative referred to signifies purposelessness on the part of god. The import of all these arguments, the Jaina philosopher maintains is that accounting for the existence of god is an absolutely hopeless task and the better alternative is to dispense with the supposition altogether.[11]

Jacobi explains how the atheistic aspects of Jaina thought can be understood in its proper perspective when he writes: "Though the Jainas are undoubtedly atheistical, as we understand the term, still they would probably object to being styled atheists. While admitting that the world is without beginning or end, and therefore not produced by a god, or ruled by one, they recognize a highest deity (*paramadevata*) as the object of veneration, viz., the *Jīna,* the teacher of the Sacred Law, who, being absolutely free from all passions and delusion, and being possessed of omniscience, has reached absolute prefection after having annihilated all his *karma.*"[12]

The *Jīnas*, rather than the gods are thus worshipped and offered worship in temples, but since the *Jīnas* have transcended the worldly plane, they cannot really answer the prayers. Gods, who are supposed to watch and control true discipline (*sasanadhisthayika devatas*) hear and answer the prayers. It is in this sense that the erection of temples is justified. Underlying all the ceremonial worship in temples and erection of statues for the *Jīnas* is the strong conviction

[11] See S.N. Dasgupta, *op. cit.*, pp. 204-206

[12] *Encyclopaedia of Religion & Ethics*, Vol. 11, p. 187

of the Jaina that the best mode of worshipping them is to practise the *Jīna's* discipline.

We may conclude that Jaina 'atheism', without denying the existence of the soul and without presuming a creator makes each individual responsible for his own fate and maintains that everything in the universe is eternal and that ethical living alone can ensure lasting happiness.

PART II

EPISTEMOLOGY

7

Jaina Epistemology : An Over-view

KNOWLEDGE in general is analysable into ideas,—ideas about things of the external world, about other men and about one's own self. The ideas about every one of the three categories mentioned above constitute knowledge only when they have all been systematized and absorbed by the 'subject', the knower. It will at once be noticed that not all ideas are of the same value and validity. This is evident from our reference to some ideas as true and some others as false. The awareness of such a distinction between true and false knowledge, what is also referred to as valid and invalid knowledge, presupposes an enquiry into the origin and validity of all knowledge. The study whose concern is a systematic reflection about knowledge, a reflection which is solely centred round knowledge itself is *epistemology*.

Since knowledge presupposes also a knower and the object of knowledge, while analysing *how* the knower knows the known, the *means* of knowledge requires to be analysed and understood. The means of knowledge are referred to as *pramāṇas* and the objects of knowledge are known as the *prameyas* in Indian epistemology. The first systematic treatment of the *pramāṇas* is found in Gautama's *Nyāya-Sūtra* which deals also with *prameya*. Later the study of knowledge was gradually separated from that of the objects of knowledge. This gave rise to works on pure logic and epistemology.

This tendency is first noticeable in the works of the Jaina and the Buddhist philosophers. The evidence from the Jaina tradition is found in the *Bhagavatī-Sūtra* in which Lord Mahāvīra is referred to as saying : "There are four means of valid knowledge (*pramāṇas*), perception (*pratyakṣa*), inference (*anumāna*), analogy (*upamāna*), and authority (*āgama*). . ."[1] Generally we find these four *pramāṇas* accepted in the Jaina philosophy, but sometimes we find only three *pramāṇas* being mentioned. For example, the *Sthānāṅga-Sūtra* maintains that there are three *pramāṇas* only, perception, authority and inference.[2] Though these discussions in the Jaina classics point to the fact that the Jaina philosophers did believe in independently considering the *pramāṇās*, it should not be understood that the Jaina canons maintained strictly the distinction between the categories and means of valid knowledge. We find them both to be related as well as synthesized in many of the Jaina works. We find for example a complete identification of the two — referred to as *jñāna* and *pramāṇa* in the *Tattvārtha-Sūtra*. The author of the *Sūtra* declares : "*Jñāna* is of five varieties, viz., *mati*, *śruta*, *avadhi*, *manaḥparyāya* and *kevala*. All these varieties are *pramāṇa*."[3] He took right knowledge as *pramāṇa*.

Of the five types of knowledge *mati* and *śruta* are referred to as *parokṣa* (mediate or indirect)[4] and *avadhi*, *manaḥparyāya* and *kevala* are referred to as *pratyakṣa* (immediate or direct).[5]

Mati-jñāna stands for determinate knowledge derived through the sense organs and the mind. *Śruta-jñāna* signifies knowledge derived through words which are symbols of thought, gestures, etc. It is significant that the Jaina tradition considers *mati* and *śruta* as including within them all the six sources of knowledge recognized in the Mīmāṁsa system, viz., inference (*anumāna*), similarity (*upamāna*), verbal testimony (*āgama*), implication (*arthāpatti*), probability (*sambhava*) and negation (*abhāva*).[6] The definition of verbal testimony as "knowledge arising from words, which taken in their proper acceptance, express reality not inconsistent with what is established by direct knowledge"[7] offers us an insight into the deeper significance of *śruta* we find in the Jaina tradition in addition to

[1] V. 43. 192

[2] 185

[3] I. 9-10; Cf. *Bhagavatī-Sūtra*, 88.2.317 which refers to the five types of knowledge as *abhinībodhika*, *śruta*, *avadhi*, *manaḥparyāya* and *kevala*.

[4] *Tattvārtha-Sūtra*, I. 11

[5] *Ibid.*, I. 12

[6] See *Tattvārtha-Sūtra bhāṣya*, I. 12

[7] *Nyāyāvatāra*, 5

pointing to the integrated nature of the various sources of knowledge. *Avadhi-jñāna* is determinate knowledge of physical objects derived directly by the knower without the instrumentality of either the sense organs or the mind. *Manaḥparyāya* refers to the knowledge of other minds, i. e., the thoughts of the others. *Kevala-jñāna* is the determinate and unlimited knowledge of the whole of Reality that the individual derives directly.

In some of the later Jaina philosophers we find pointed discussion regarding how the validity (sometimes referred to as the rightness) of knowledge itself could be determined. Valid knowledge is considered to be knowledge which illumines itself as well as others. Knowledge in this sense is compared to a lamp which, by its being lighted, reveals not only objects external to it but reveals itself also. One of the Jaina philosophers, Siddhasena defines *pramāṇa* as that knowledge which is free from obstruction (*bādhavivarjita*) and which illumines itself and other things (*svaparābhāsi*).[8] The same author points out that *pramāṇa*, by its very nature, is to be taken to be free from error. To say that *pramāṇa* is erroneous (*bhrānta*) is to introduce a contradiction.[9] Digressing a little, it may be pointed out that such a position taken by the Jaina philosophers points to their realistic standpoint. The argument is that since it has not been proved that the whole world of appearance is a matter of error, *pramāṇa* as revealing itself and other things points to the reality of both.[10] The definition of error (*viparyaya*) as that which is opposite of knowledge and as consisting in the failure to distinguish between that which is and which is not (*sad-asator aviśeṣād*)[11] points to a realistic theory of knowledge. It also signifies that all *pramāṇa* is *jñāna* but not all *jñāna* is *pramāṇa*.

The acceptance of internal as well as external validity of knowledge by the Jainas is diametrically opposed to the theories held by the Yogācāra Buddhists, the Nyāya philosophers and the Mīmāṁsakas. The Yogācāra Buddhists believed that knowledge illumines itself alone, since, according to them there are no external objects. The Naiyāyikas and Mīmāṁsakas held that knowledge has the power to reveal the external objects alone as it cannot reveal itself.

8 *Ibid.*, 1
9 *Ibid.*, 6
10 *Ibid.*, 7
11 See *Tattvārtha-Sūtra*, I. 32 & 33 and the *bhāṣya*

We are able to discern clearly three stages through which the Jaina theory of knowledge has been evolved. We have already referred to the first stage. In this stage knowledge is classified into five types. The five-fold division is pre-canonical in origin. N. Tatia points out that the *Āgama* theory of knowledge is very old and probably originated in the pre-Mahāvīra period.[12] So it can be surmised that Mahāvīra accepted the scheme of knowledge from the Pārśva tradition he inherited.

In the second stage we find only two broad divisions of knowledge, immediate and mediate (*pratyakṣa* and *parokṣa*). The scheme is found in the *Sthānāṅga-Sūtra*.[13] In the *Tattvārtha-Sūtra* knowledge is first divided into five types and then these are grouped into two—*pratyakṣa* and *parokṣa*. In the second phase *mati* and *śruta* were considered to be *parokṣa* and the other three as *pratyakṣa*.[14] We also find the view that in accordance with the objects known by means of *pramāṇa* it is either direct knowledge (*pratyakṣa*) or indirect knowledge (*parokṣa*). The *Nyāyāvatāra* refers to direct knowledge as that which takes cognizance of objects which are not beyond the senses and indirect knowledge as that which is of a different kind.

Pratyakṣa is defined by Umāsvāti (the author of the *Tattvārtha-Sūtra*) as valid knowledge directly derived by the *jīva* without the help of any of the five sense organs or the mind. We find another definition of direct knowledge : "The perfect manifestation of the innate nature of a soul, emerging on the total annihilation of all obstructive veils is called direct perception."[15] It is significant that by the annihilation of the various types of *karma* obstructing the acquisition of knowledge, the true nature of the 'knower' becomes manifest, that too, without the instrumentality of the sense organs and the mind. This is in the truest spirit of Jainism, *pratyakṣa* proper and, as a *pramāṇa*, it is not dependent on anything else but is completely self-dependent.[16]

[12] *Studies in Jaina Philosophy* (Banaras : Jain Cultural Research Society, 1951), p. 27

[13] II. 1. 7

[14] I. 11 & 12

[15] *Parīkṣāmukha-Sūtra*, II. 1-4; III. 1-2; *Pramāṇanayatattvālokālaṅkāra*, II. 2-3

[16] We have earlier indicated the middle position that the Jaina philosopher takes in regard to the function of knowledge.

Direct or Immediate perception proper is *Kevala-jñāna* and it is characterized as pure and perfect. But since there are stages of attaining such perfect knowledge[17] these are also referred to as immediate perception, in a qualified sense. These are *Avadhi-jñāna* and *Manaḥparyāya-jñāna. Pratyakṣa* is also referred to as *pāramārthika* (transcendental) as against *parokṣa* which is referred to also as *vyāvahārika* (empirical). The term *pratyakṣa* is appended to both the terms *pāramārthika* and *vyāvahārika* to indicate the type of perception resulting without the aid of the sense organs and the mind (*pāramārthika-pratyakṣa*) and the perception resulting from the activity of the sense organs (*vyāvahāra-pratyakṣa*).[18]

Parokṣa is defined as "other than *pratyakṣa.*"[19] Since *pratyakṣa* as discussed above relates to knowledge dependent on the self alone, *parokṣa* as "other than *pratyakṣa*" signifies knowledge which is dependent on the sense organs (*indriyas*) and the mind (*manas*). *Parokṣa-jñāna* understood as empirical knowledge is defined as that which is conditioned by the senses and the mind and is limited. In terms of this two-fold division, inference (*anumāna*), analogy (*upamāna*) and verbal testimony (*śabda*) are all classified under *parokṣa.*

Knowledge derived through the sense organs and the mind was thus considered indirect by the Jaina philosophers and this was directly against the view held by the other schools of Indian philosophy which *generally* held the view that the sense organs give us immediate or direct knowledge whereas all the other 'sources' lead to only indirect or mediate knowledge.

In the third stage of the evolution of Jaina epistemology perception is considered as giving direct knowledge (for practical purpose) though it is still maintained that knowledge derived through the

[17] There is a clear suggestion in *Nyāyāvatāra*, 28 for this concept of 'degrees of knowledge'. The result of *pramāṇa* is stated to be the removal of ignorance (*ajñāna-nivartanā*), of *kevala-jñāna,*— bliss and equanimity and of other kinds of knowledge, — selection and rejection of objects.

[18] See *Nyāyāvatāra* along with *vṛtti* on verse 27. There is no contradiction involved in the division of *pratyakṣa* itself into two as indicated above after referring to *pratyakṣa* as *pāramārthika* and *parokṣa* as *vyāvahārika* since the spirit of Jaina epistemology requires us to understand that from the point of view of the unbounded possibilities of the human self no external aids are required to 'produce knowledge' since the self in its pristine purity is identical with knowledge.

[19] *Nyāyāvatāra*, 4

mind is indirect. This phase in the evolution of the Jaina theory of knowledge was characterized by its falling in line with the other schools of Indian philosophy, by considering sense-perception as giving *pratyakṣa-jñāna* or direct knowledge.[20] In terms of the Jaina usage — *mati* and *śruta* began to be called *pratyakṣa* as they were possible through the operation of the sense organs. The *Tattvārtha-Sūtra* refers to this as *saṁvyavahārika-pratyakṣa*.[21] Mohan Lal Mehta maintains that the third stage was influenced by the general tendency of Indian philosophy that regards sensory knowledge as direct. He points out that the later Jaina logicians and philosophers also took this view in the name of *laukika-pratyakṣa*. The gist of the third stage, according to him is : *Avadhi*, *manaḥparyāya* and *kevala-jñāna* are really direct; *śruta-jñāna* is always indirect; *mati-jñāna* produced by the sense organs is really indirect but is regarded as direct for practical purposes; and *mati-jñāna* produced by the mind is always indirect.[22]

In conclusion we may add that the distinguishing feature of Jaina epistemology is that in its strictest sense there is one and only one type of immediate and real knowledge and that is *kevala-jñāna*. It is because of this that such a type of knowledge is also referred to as transcendental and extra-sensory perception. Since the function of the sense organs and the mind are considered to be positive obstructions to knowledge, *avadhi-jñāna* and *manaḥparyāya-jñāna* are referred to as direct perceptions only in a qualified sense, viz., as representing the progressive stages towards and as preparatory steps to direct knowledge, *kevala-jñāna*. Since the ultimate criterion of real knowledge is absence of obstruction and since one of the obstructive factors, the mind is found in *avadhi* and *manaḥparyāya* they are considered as not being capable of giving direct knowledge.

20 See *Nandi-Sūtra*, 4

21 I. 9-12

22 See *Outlines of Jaina Philosophy* (Bangalore : Jain Mission Society, 1954), p. 89

8

Darsana and Jnana

BEFORE considering the various types of knowledge according to the Jaina tradition it is essential that we consider the two stages through which knowledge itself is acquired. If the term knowledge is considered to stand for *jñāna*, the preliminary step to it, the initiation into it, is *darśana.* The Jaina philosophers make use of the term *darśana* and *jñāna* to represent respectively the indeterminate and the determinate phases in the process of getting knowledge.

The sense-object contact which initiates the process of knowledge first stirs consciousness and in this stage there is a mere awareness of the presence of the object. As such there is only an indefinite and indistinct idea about the object in question. The details about the object are not perceived and naturally there is no question of identifying the object as belonging to a particular class or group. In the Jaina terminology, the first stage is referred to as the Apprehension-stage (*darśana*) and in it cognition contains only existence (*sattāmātra*) as its content.

The process of analysis which is inherent in the human mind enables the conversion of mere sense-awareness into sense-perception. The vague consciousness of the object presented to the senses is replaced by a definite comprehension of the class-characteristics of it. The distinctness of the object is grasped and this paves the way for a further expansion of the domain of knowledge.

The two stages of *darśana* and *jñāna* may be described as 'knowledge by acquiantance' and 'knowledge-about' since in the first there is only the contact of the object with the mind perceiving it and in the second, there is a mental comprehension of the details about the quality and class of the object. The passage from *darśana* to *jñāna* may be referred to as a passage from the raw, unverbalized stage in acquiring knowledge to a stage in which language can be employed to clearly indicate the various elements that have all been synthesized to form the core of knowledge. This distinction is generally agreed to by all the Jaina philosophers, though emphasis on the one or the other aspects of the dichotomy make for different expressions of the same fundamental position. This will be evident when we turn to specific philosophers.

Vīrasena defines *jñāna* as the comprehension of both the generic and specific qualities of the external objects. When the self turns inwards and introspects it 'knows' itself and this is referred to as *darśana* by him. *Darśana* is hence considered *antarmukha* (turned inside, introvert) while *jñāna* is described as *bahirmukha* (turned outside, extrovert). It is evident, he does not accept the simple distinction in terms of apprehension of generic qualities and comprehension of specific characteristics. The reason he gives is that it is logically not possible to conceive of the general without considering the particular and *vice versa.* Particularity without generality is a figment and generality without particularity is an impossibility, according to him.[1]

In keeping with this logical stand he refers to objects of knowledge as 'complexes.' Even the simplest case of perception denotes the comprehension of the complex of the universal and particular characteristics presented to the senses by the object in question. Though the object as a synthesis of the generic and specific qualities is presented to the subject, i. e., the perceiving mind, in the first stage of *darśana,* there is only an introspective understanding of the object. This facilitates analysis and synthesis and, in the second stage of *jñāna* there is a comprehension of the selfsame objects as belonging to the external world, occupying particular places, as having existence in a specific point of time, as belonging to a particular class and as sharing certain qualities in common with the other members of the class, etc. In the comprehension stage, therefore there is the outward turning of the mind to 'get at' and understand reality.

1 See his commentary Dhavala on *Ṣatkhaṅḍāgama* of Puṣpadanta, I. 1. 4

Brahmadeva holds a similar view. According to him the cognition of one's own self, consisting in the striving for the origination of comprehension in its wake, is apprehension and the subsequent cognition of external objects is comprehension.[2] Tatia gives a clear exposition of Brahmadeva's position when he writes: "The soul knows as well as intuits much in the same way as fire burns and illumines. The selfsame consciousness is called *darśana* as well as *jñāna* with reference to the difference of its object. It is called *darśana* when it is engaged in intuiting the self, and *jñāna* when engaged in knowing the non-self. Knowledge would lose its validity if it were admitted that *darśana* and *jñāna* are confined to the comprehension respectively of the universal and the particular exclusively."[3]

The introvert and the extrovert elements in Vīrasena's theory are thus accepted *in toto* by Brahmadeva though he, unlike Vīrasena, is not critical of the simpler classification of the universal and particular. He specifically points out that for those whose intellects are sharp the distinction may be meaningful and exhaustive; but for those who are not capable of a sharper analysis the distinction between the self-conscious and the other-conscious states perceivable in the development of knowledge is much more significant. In Brahmadeva's view the true import of the Jaina scriptures lies in the higher analysis of the complex whole that the object is.

Nemicandra does not accept the above distinction. He prefers to consider apprehension as acquiring knowledge of the general characteristics of the objects without knowing their particularities and comprehension as knowledge in which details about the objects are also grasped.[4]

Vādideva refers to apprehension itself as consisting of two stages. In the first stage there is mere awareness of the object presented to consciousness. In the second, there is an apprehension of the general features of the objects and this is referred to as *avagraha* and as constituting the first stage in comprehension or *jñāna*.[5] Comprehension proper consists in a more systematic analysis of the objects of knowledge and of 'establishing the missing links.' In a

2 Comm. on *Dravya-saṅgraha*, 44

3 N. Tatia, *op. cit.*, p. 73

4 *Dravya-saṅgraha*, 43

5 *Pramāṇanayatattvālokālaṅkāra*, II. 7

sense, therefore, Vādideva analyses the process of getting knowledge into three stages, though he includes it within the general frame-work of apprehension and comprehension.

Hemacandra expresses the organic relationship between the two stages of knowledge in a different way. He considers apprehension as being transformed into comprehension.[6] Apprehension is considered by him as the raw material of knowledge which is 'worked up' by the mind and hence as being instrumental to comprehension. The term comprehension connotes an understanding of the distinctive qualities of the object. He defines Apprehension as "the cognition of our object which does not take into account specific determinations." Comprehension is not something which is entirely new and unrelated to Apprehension. So we have comprehension when the generic qualities are understood as generic features and apprehension when the specific features are understood as specific features. Both are present from the beginning and so comprehension is only the actualizing of the potentiality that is apprehension.

When Apprehension and Comprehension are referred to as stages of getting knowledge the question arises whether there is a temporal relationship between the two. In this context we find three views being expressed by the Jaina philosophers. The canonical position is that these two cannot occur simultaneously. The reason held is that two conscious activities cannot occur simultaneously in the human mind. The whole controversy regarding the simultaneity or otherwise of the occurrence of Apprehension and Comprehension is only with respect to a perfected person, the *Kevala-jñāni*. Regarding the imperfect man there is no controversy at all.

The three views held are : (1) that Apprehension and Comprehension occur simultaneously (2) that they occur successively and (3) that there is complete identity between the two.

(1) The first is the canonical position and the main argument put forward for this position is that in the perfected man the Apprehension-obscuring *karma* (*darśanāvaraṇa-karma*) as well as Comprehension-obscuring *karma* (*jñānāvaraṇa-karma*) are both destroyed and since the obstructions are completely removed, *darśana* and *jñāna* must both be simultaneous. Moreover, if Appre-

[6] See comm. on *Pramāṇa-mīmāṁsā*, I. 1. 26

hension and Comprehension are considered to occur simultaneously, omniscience itself would be conditional and not unconditional, a position which is just opposed to the spirit of the Jaina conception of *kevala-jñāna.*

(2) The second view puts forward a logical argument against the first. "If perfect apprehension and perfect comprehension were to occur simultaneously, what is the point in recognizing two separate veils of *karma,*—the apprehension-veiling and comprehension-veiling ?" The view also points to the psychological impossibility of two things being comprehended simultaneously. These difficulties are got over by maintaining that apprehension and comprehension can occur only one after another. This view seems to account for advancement in general—whether in knowledge or in ethical life. The earlier stage is necessarily transcended in the later. Epistemologically, the advanced stage in knowledge connotes the earlier elementary stage having been completed. Ethically—and more specifically in terms of the 'veils of *karma*',—advancement entails the various veils being removed one after the other when, finally, all the veils are removed and perfection is attained.

(3) The third view refers to the fact that in the perfected man the senses and the mind do not serve any useful purpose. This means there is no separate faculty for apprehension. From this it is evident that in the perfected man, if at all we are to think of an apprehension and a comprehension, it can be only in terms of an identity between the two. It is understandable therefore that this view concedes the distinctness of apprehension and comprehension upto the level of *manaḥparyāya-jñāna* but not in *kevala-jñāna.*

Reviewing the three alternatives it may be pointed out that there does not seem to be much difference between (1) and (3) inasmuch as they both are critical of (2). The view that two conscious activities cannot take place simultaneously is acceptable and it is interesting to note that both (2) and (3) point this out.

All the same the truth in the succession theory cannot be ignored since it points the way in which omniscience itself is to be analysed and understood. However, 'succession' in the omniscient himself seems to be a difficult point to concede. The identity-concept contained in the third theory is acceptable since *in the omniscient* simultaneous occurrence itself would mean occurrence of something not known before, and this amounts to admitting an element of ignorance in him.

One of the Jaina thinkers, Yaśovijaya points to the elements of truth inherent in the three theories as follows : "He who admits separate identity of apprehension and comprehension but does not recognize succession, is right from the *empirical* standpoint that entertains distinction, the believer in the successive occurrence of apprehension and comprehension is correct from the *analytic* standpoint that distinguishes the border-line between cause and effect, while the upholder of the identity of apprehension and comprehension is right from the *synthetic* standpoint that tends to abolish distinction and establish identity. Therefore none of the three propositions can be called improper."[7]

[7] Cited in M.L. Mehta, *Jaina Psychology* (Amritsar : Sohanlal Jaindharma Pracharak Samiti, 1955), p. 56.

9

Mati-jnana

MATI-*jñāna* is defined as "knowledge caused by the senses and the mind."[1] In the Jaina works we find mention being made of two varieties of *mati-jñāna*—one derived through the working of the five sense organs and the other resulting from the activity of the mind. Some commentators add a third variety, that due to the joint activity of the senses and the mind. The two varieties mentioned above probably signify the important roles played respectively by the sense organs and the mind, for, it is difficut to conceive of knowledge in which the sense organs or the mind has not played a part. This is not to deny the *kevala-jñāna* concept of the Jainas, but it is to point out here that *in the context of* a discussion of the various stages of evolution of perceptual knowledge the role of either the sense organs or the mind cannot be overlooked or ignored completely. In support of our argument we point to the various 'stages' in *mati* discussed by the Jaina philosophers—*avagraha* (cognition of sense data), *īha* (speculation) *apāya* or *avāya* (perceptual judgment) and *dhāraṇa* (retention).

Avagraha : This is considered to develop through two stages : *vyañjanāvagraha* (contact-awareness) and *arthāvagraha* (object-comprehension).[2] In the first stage the object in question comes into contact with the particular sense organ by means of a transformation of its substance into the sense-data perceivable by the

1 *Tattvārtha-Sūtra*, I. 14
2 *Nandi-Sūtra*, 27; *Tattvārtha-Sūtra*, I. 17-18

relevant organ. For example, auditory perception requires first that the *auditory sensations* reach the ear and establish a 'sense-contact' with it. The auditory sensations result from a transformation of the source of the sound, the object, into sound waves which reach the ear, and through the nerves stimulate consciousness. Then the sensations lead to their being identified as specific types of sensations. The *vyañjanāvagraha* stage is often considered as a necessary preliminary step leading to *arthāvagraha* and the latter as the consummation of the former. Contact-awareness is considered to be possible only with regard to four of the five sense organs, the eyes being excluded. *Arthāvagraha* is considered to be of six varieties resulting from the activity of the five sense organs and the mind.

The *avagraha* stage is considered to be instantaneous but the view that this refers to the *arthāvagraha* stage and not to the *vyañjanāvagraha* stage is also found. The reason is obvious. In the *vyañjanāvagraha* stage sensations (of different types) are said to constantly impinge on the sense organ concerned as a result of which alone there is the stimulation of consciousness. Only at a particular level there is the *actual stirring of consciousness.* As the sensations require a definite time-duration for their successfully 'waking up' consciousness, the first stage is not considered to be instantaneous. In the Jaina terminology : countless number of instants lapse before the sensations are 'effective'. The moment consciousness is stirred up there is the object-comprehension. It is hence considered that *arthāvagraha* is not instantaneous. The question whether *arthāvagraha* is determinate or indeterminate has been debated but it is not relevant here when we analyse the different stages through which *mati-jñāna* is evolved.

Īha : The stimulation of consciousness (produced by *vyañjanāvagraha*) leads to the dawning of awareness (*arthāvagraha*) and hence the line of demarcation between the two is thin and imperceptible ; this might have been one reason why there has been so much of difference of opinion among the Jaina philosophers in regard to the exact nature of *avagraha.*

The next stage in the evolution of perceptual knowledge, logically as well as psychologically, is the mind working upon the sensation it has received, thanks to the stirring of consciousness. This is refered to as *īha* or the speculative stage. In this stage there is an attempt to know *more* about the sensation that has been supplied. For example in the previous stage of *avagraha* there was only a general awareness of sound, the awareness itself having resulted from the sound atoms saturating the auditory organ. The general awareness was in regard to the fact that it was the sound sensation, not visual or other types of sensations which were at the back of the stirring of consciousness. The awareness becoming *more distinct* signifies the *activity of the mind* (here referred to as *īha*) which wants to know precisely the nature of the sound—whether it was, for example, the one produced by a conch or a bell or a trumpet. The Jaina philosophers are all agreed that in *īha* there is the passage from the general awareness to a specific enquiry regarding the sensation received. We find however the same truth being expressed in different ways.

The *Nandi-Sūtra* refers to the distinctive feature of *īha* by differentiating it from *avagraha* : "In sensation a person hears a sound, but does not know whose sound it is, whereas in speculation he cognizes the nature of the sound."[3] The attempt of the mind to comprehend the specific nature of the sensation in the stage of *īha* is pointed to by another Jaina classic when it says : "Sensation cognizes only a part of the object, while speculation cognizes the rest and strives for the determination of a specific feature."[4] Since the significance of *īha* in terms of the above definitions is that there is fresh effort to understand the nature of the sensations produced, we find a Jaina philosopher making a pointed reference to this when he defines *īha* as "the striving for a specific determination of the object that has already been cognized by sensation."[5] In this definition the term object does not refer to the physical object in question but to the object of consciousness, the sensation under analysis. Identification of the 'source', the object from which the sensation emanates, belongs to the next stage, the *apāya* stage, and should not be understood as belonging to the second stage.

It is significant that the Jaina philosophers have carefully distinguished between speculation (*īha*) and doubt (*saṁśaya*). Doubt is defined as the mental state in which mutually contradictory objects are pressing for recognition ; the mind's incapacity to

3 *Nandi-Sūtra*, 35

4 *Tattvārtha-Sūtra bhāṣya*, I. 15

5 *Pūjyapāda Devānandi*, *Sarvārthasiddhi*, I. 15

exclude the false from the true results in the absence of determination. Speculation, on the other hand, represents the mind's successful attempt, through cogent reasoning and methodical analysis, to distinguish clearly between the true and the false.[6]

Apāya : This is the stage when the 'alternatives' have been examined and one of them is affirmed, by denying the others. It is hence referred to as the stage of determinate cognition. The existent qualities are affirmed and the non-existent ones are excluded. In the example cited previously, the stage of *īha* characterizes the mind's trying to identify the source of the sound. This involved an analysis of the various possibilities. The sound might have emanated from a conch or a bell, etc. Whereas sweetness characterizes the sound emanating from a conch, harshness is the distinctive quality of the sound produced when a bell is rung. From the presence of one of these qualities in the sound speculated about, the source is precisely determined.

Logically the stage of *apāya* is described as incorporating a perceptual judgment. The perceptual judgment in the example takes the form : "This must be the sound of a conch." The *Sarvārthasiddhi* defines *apāya* as "cognition of the true nature on account of the cognition of the particular characteristics."[7]

A slightly different opinion is held by some Jaina philosophers who maintain that the stage of *apāya* signifies only an elimination of the non-existent characteristics and that positive affirmation of the existent qualities takes place only in the next stage, the *dhāraṇa* stage. This view is criticised by the rival school as absurd. The basis of the criticism is that in the very process of denying certain qualities, certain other qualities are affirmed. The view insisting that affirmation of positive qualities belongs to the stage of *apāya* seems to be more logically consistent with the general theory of knowledge of the Jainas, that when the obstructive elements are removed, knowledge automatically dawns.

Dhāraṇa : The evolution of perceptual knowledge is completed in this stage. The perceptual judgment arrived at in the third stage is to be retained if it is at all to become perception proper. The fact of retention of the judgment is the distinctive feature of *dhāraṇa*.

[6] See *Viśeṣāvaśyaka-bhāṣya*, 183-184

[7] *Sarvārthasiddhi*, I. 15

Knowledge in general may be described as a system in which judgments of various types and on various matters have been co-ordinated, with the result that when a new piece of knowledge is received—to start with, it is only a sensation—it is interpreted in the light of knowledge already possessed, interpreted as belonging to or relatable to the domain of knowledge already possessed. One of the aims of perceiving therefore may be considered as retaining in memory what has already been 'learnt'. It is in this sense that *dhāraṇa* or retention is considered to be the consummation of perceptual knowledge. The *Nandi-Sūtra* defines *dhāraṇa* as the act of retaining a perceptual judgment for a number of instants.[8] In the *Tattvārtha-Sūtra bhāṣya* of Umāswāmi we find a three-fold analysis of *dhāraṇa*. In the first stage there is a positive determination of the qualities of the objects of comprehension, in the second there is the retention of the comprehension and in the third there is the ability to recognize the same on future occasions.[9] The soundness of the view from the point of view of the psychology of perception is especially striking, for, retention, if it is to be of any use at all in knowledge must involve also the ability of the mind to recall it and recalling will be possible only when there is the recognition of an idea newly received, as belonging to a class (or even as not belonging to a specific class) already known to the individual. Another philosopher, Jīnabhadra holds a similar view. He analyses *dhāraṇa* to be constituted of three aspects, the absence of lapse (*avicyuti*), the resultant emergence of mental trace (*vāsana*) and the recollection of it in the future (*anusmaraṇa*).[10]

Some Jaina philosophers define *dhāraṇa* as the condition of recollection but the definition meets with the criticism that it is untrue to human psychology inasmuch as it involves the position that the perceptual judgment is retained up to the time of recollection. This criticism also points out that according to the new theory no other cognition will be possible during the interval between the formation of the perceptual judgment and its recollection. The criticism is a valid one since both the schools are agreed that two cognitions cannot be had simultaneously.

8 *Nandi-Sūtra*, 35

9 *Tattvārtha-Sūtra bhāṣya*, I.15

10 *Viśeṣāvaśyaka-bhāṣya*, 291

It may be pointed out that the four stages of perception analysed by the Jaina philosophers are comparable to the analysis given by modern psychologists. The psychological insight of the Jaina philosophers is extremely significant of their carefully and deeply analysing concepts relating to the human mind.

10

Sruta-jnana

THE term *śruta-jñāna* stands for scriptural or verbal knowledge and is derived from two terms—*śru* which means 'to hear' and *jñāna* which stands for knowledge. *Śruta-jñāna* is a kind of *parokṣa-jñāna* and it is obvious why it is so. It is the knowledge which is derived not directly but indirectly,—through the scriptures and through the reliable words of others who are well-informed about the knowledge they are imparting. In this context Tatia makes a significant point when he explains the conditions to be fulfilled for getting *śruta-jñāna*. He writes : "Knowledge of the conventional vocabulary and conscious application of it are the conditions of *śruta-jñāna*. In other words, conscious exercise of the gift of language is the indispensable condition of *śruta-jñāna*. The cognitions which, in spite of their being couched in words, do not involve conscious attempt on the part of the cognizer at application of vocabulary, fall in the category of *mati-jñāna* (sensuous cognition) and not *śruta-jñāna*."[1]

In the Jaina tradition *śruta-jñāna* originally meant "knowledge contained in the scriptures."[2] It gradually came to signify also "knowledge of the scriptures." It is of two kinds : *aṅgabāhya* (not incorporated in the twelve *Aṅgas*) and *aṅgapraviṣṭa* (incorporated in the twelve *Aṅgas*). There are twelve varieties of the first kind and the second is of more than twelve varieties.[3] In another sense

[1] *Studies in Jaina Philosophy*, pp. 49-50

[2] *Sthānāṅga-Sūtra*, 71

[3] *Tattvārtha-Sūtra bhāṣya*, I. 20

there are an infinite number of *śrutas*, corresponding to the number of letters and their combinations. According to *Āvaśyakaniryukti* it is not possible to specify the number of *śrutas* since they are as many as the number of letters and their various combinations. Fourteen salient characteristics are however enumerated in the work. These are *akṣara* (alphabet), *saṁjñin* (cognitive), *samyak* (right), *sādika* (having beginning), *saparyavasita* (having end), *gamika* (containing repetitions) and *aṅgapraviṣṭa* (included in the original scripture) with their opposites, viz., *anakṣara*, *asaṁjñin*, etc.[5] A detailed treatment of these, however, is not found in the work. It is in the *Nandi-Sūtra* that we have a clear and detailed indication of the fourteen characteristics of *śruta*.[6] Of these only four along with their opposites are philosophically significant and hence we shall refer to them alone here.

Akṣaraśruta is divided into three, corresponding to the shape of the letter (*saṁjñākṣara*), sound of the letter (*vyañjanākṣara*) and *śruta-jnāna* proper derivable through the five sense organs and the mind (*labdhyakṣaras*). The first two, it is obvious, deal with material symbols, used in writing the script and in using the spoken word respectively. Hence they are called *dravya-śruta*. The third one is referred to as *bhāvaśruta*.

Saṁjñi-śruta is analysed into three types corresponding to the three types of cognitival activity : (1) discursive thinking that takes into account the past, the present and the future ; (2) consciousness of the present resulting in the capacity for discriminating between the right and wrong types of activity for the preservation and destruction of life respectively ; and (3) consciousness due to knowledge of the right scriptures.[8]

Samyak-śruta refers to the Jaina source-books like *Ācārāṅga*, *Sūtrakṛtāṅga*, etc. whereas the non-Jaina source-books like the Vedas and the Epics are the *mithyā-śrutas*.

Asaṁjñi-śruta is also divided into three, corresponding to the type of mind involved, viz., the under-developed mind, the totally

[4] 17, 18
[5] 19
[6] *Nandi-Sūtra*, 38
[7] *Ibid.*, 39
[8] *Ibid*

undeveloped mind (instinctive type) and the perverted mind (believing in false scriptures).

Śruta-jnāna is considered to be superior to *mati-jñāna* since the latter deals with the present alone, that of the objects existing at the time of sensual and mental comprehension whereas the former is concerned with the past, present and the future. In this sense the scriptures contain wisdom which is eternally true. Hence also "*Śruta-jñāna* may be said to embody the highest and the most advanced knowledge arrived at by the most perfect form of *mati-jñāna*. It is based on *mati-jñāna* and consists in truths, discovered, developed and revealed by the most perfect of the rational souls. It is a system of scriptural truths, the holiness of which is unimpeccable. *Śruta-jñāna* is thus authoritative knowledge, the validity of which is unchallengeable."[9]

The significance of *śruta* as stated above becomes clear from Kunda Kundācārya's division of it into four classes, viz., *labdhi* or Integration, *bhāvana* or Consideration, *upayoga* or Understanding and *naya* or Interpretation.[10] Rather than considering these as four classes of *śruta-jñāna*, as Bhattacharya suggests, "it is far more reasonable to look upon these processes as four steps to the progressive explanation of a phenomenon than as so many independent and mutually exclusive kinds of scriptural knowledge."[11]

If the utility of *śruta-jñāna* is to be fully realized and if it consists in enabling man to apply the accumulated mass of knowledge to interpret and understand the phenomena around him, it is understandable how every one of the four steps represents the progressive stages of the interpretative ability he gets.

Labdhi stands for the stage of explanation which needs reference to a phenomenon with which the one under consideration is associated. If the two phenomena are named X and Y, since these two are known to be associated with each other, the nature of Y, the new phenomenon can easily be determined by dwelling on the nature of X.

Bhāvana is the stage of reconsidering the nature of the familiar phenomenon (X) so that the new phenomenon (Y) which is

[9] H. S. Bhattacharya, *Reals in the Jaina Metaphysics* (Bombay : The Seth Santi Das Khetsy Charitable Trust, 1966), pp. 300-301

[10] *Pañcāstikāya, samayasāra*, 43

[11] *op. cit.*, p. 301

known to be associated with the old one can be understood properly.

Upayoga is the stage where there is a proper understanding of the new phenomenon, thanks to the process of integration and consideration which have gone into the attempt at comprehending it in the light of an already familiar phenomenon.

A very interesting parallel is drawn between the fourth stage (*naya*) in the *śruta-jñāna* and the fourth stage (*dhāraṇa*) in the *mati-jñāna*. *Dhāraṇa*, consisting as it does the mental retention of a precept, is practically the extreme limit of the sensuous *mati-jñāna*. In the same manner, *naya* which consists in the explanation of a phenomenon by emphasizing its particular aspect, is the farthest limit of *śruta-jñāna*. This is because the significance of *naya* consists not so much in referring to the accumulated mass of knowledge (in explaining a phenomenon) as in explaining a thing by looking to its various modes and specific aspect directly.[12]

The distinctive feature of the Jaina theory of *śruta* is that it is always considered to be preceded by *mati*.[13] None of the schools of Indian philosophy which refer to knowledge derived through verbal testimony, maintains that perceptual knowledge is basic to scriptural or verbal knowledge.

The peculiar theory of the Jainas is attributable to the fact that early in their tradition *śruta* was considered as knowledge born through the sense organ of hearing. Gradually it was extended to cover knowledge acquired by all the other sense organs also. The Jaina view is that since knowledge in general, if at all it is to be useful, has to be *communicated*, and since communication is through language and since verbal expressions are directly perceived by the ears, *śruta* is always preceded by *mati*. Though verbal expressions alone are directly perceived by the ears non-verbal expressions (thoughts) are potential objects of auditory perception. Also whatever might be the type of perception experienced – visual, gustatory, tactual or olfactory – they have all to go into the thought-processes of man and eventually are convertible into linguistic expressions, sound symbols — which impinge on the auditory organs of the hearer and 'reach' him. Since the employment of words in thought

12 *Ibid.*, pp. 302-303
13 *Tattvārtha-Sūtra*, I. 20

is symptomatic of auditory cognitions and words are the necessary media through which perceptual experiences in general are communicated by others, *śruta-jñāna* is considered to be always preceded by *mati-jñāna*.

Tatia attributes the three-fold meaning of *śruta* found in the Jaina tradition (scripture, written or spoken symbol and inarticulate verbal knowledge) to the gradual subtlety of speculation that took place in the development of Jaina thought. He does not mean that the three-fold development in the meaning of *śruta* can be chronologically studied. He points out that the selfsame thinkers could have started from the conception of *śruta* as scripture and reached the conception of *śruta* as inarticulate verbal knowledge. The speculations recorded in Jaina scriptures on this subject are so rich, subtle and varied that it is difficult to ascertain the original contributions of the later Jaina authors.[14]

Regarding the relationship or otherwise of *mati* and *śruta* itself there are two opposite schools of thought. According to the one *mati* and *śruta* are entirely different from each other and, according to the other there is no distinction at all between them.

The first view is held on two grounds : (1) *Mati* is different from *śruta* in that it is not associated with words. Association with words is the characteristic feature of *śruta*. We come across two criticisms against the view. One is that if words are completely dissociated from *mati* there will be no scope at all for *īha*, *apāya* and *dhāraṇa*, for, all these involve conceptual thinking, and conceptual thinking without words is a myth. Consequently, there won't be any difference between man and animal. The second criticism is that determinate cognitions will just not be possible and we have to stop at the level of indeterminate perception.

(2) *Mati* is different from *śruta* since it can reveal its contents only to the cognizer. It is like the cognition of the dumb man who can *experience* it but *cannot express* it to others. The chief characteristic of *śruta* is that it 'flows out' and reveals its content to other cognizers. This is analogous to the man who *can talk*, who *cannot but give outward expressions to his experiences.* The view is criticised on the ground that *mati* and *śruta* as 'forms of knowledge' cannot reveal their contents to others. Even if, for the sake of argument, it is accepted that knowledge can be revealed to others, it

[14] *op. cit.*, p. 53

cannot be maintained that one is expressible and the other, not. For, in the one case expression is through words and, in the other, expression is through gestures.

The second view that *mati* and *śruta* are not distinguishable from each other is held on purely logical grounds. It is said that language does not play the determining role in *mati* and that previous knowledge is of minor consequence to *mati*. But *śruta* is said to be very much associated with words. Since every form of perception is a potential form of *śruta* it has to be maintained that perception is associated with words but free from previous knowledge. This seems to be an impossibility and hence there is no real distinction between *mati* and *śruta*. To ward off the difficulty it is suggested by the defendants of the theory of distinction that when words are absent we have *mati* and association with words transforms *mati* into *śruta*. But the critics point out that this line of demarcation is too superficial and therefore it cannot be accepted that verbal expression accords new status to knowledge. It means simply that *mati* alone is sufficient and *śruta* is superfluous. Or it may be that *śruta* itself is a case of *mati*. In that case there is no justification for treating *śruta* separately, giving it a separate 'category.' *Śruta* and *mati* must therefore be identical.

11

Kevala-Jnana

ONE of the most distinctive features of Jainism is found in its theory of *kevala-jñāna* or direct knowledge (also referred to as immediate perception). *Kevala-jñāna* is defined as perfect (*paripūrṇa*), complete (*samagra*), unique (*asādhāraṇa*), absolute (*nirapekṣa*), pure (*viśuddha*), all-comprehensive (*sarva-bhāva-jñāpaka*), that which has for its object both the world and the non-world (*lokālokaviṣaya*), and infinite (*anantaparyāya*).[1] The definition implies that the omniscient stage of man's progress in his knowledge-pursuit is the stage where Reality is intuited fully without any obstruction whatsoever. Since the fundamental position of Jainism is that the sense organs and the mind, rather than being 'sources of knowledge' are only 'sources of obstruction', it is obvious, the omniscient stage represents also the transcendence of the spatial and temporal categories. So omniscience is one wholesome experience which does not incorporate within itself limitations characteristic of experience in space and time. The superiority of *kevala-jñāna* is asserted on the ground that the objects of *mati* and *śruta* are *all* the substances, but not in all their aspects (*asarva-dravyeṣu asarva-paryāyeṣu*); of *avadhi*, only material substances, but not in all their aspects (*rupiṣveva dravyeṣu asarva pariyāyeṣu*); *manaḥparyāya* is a purer and infinitely subtle knowledge of the material substances known by *avadhi*; and *kevala* has for its object all the substances, and in all their aspects (*sarva-*

[1] *Tattvārtha-Sūtra*, I. 30 & *bhāṣya*

dravyeṣu sarva-paryāyeṣu ca).[2]

The *kevala-jñāna* concept, from the point of view of Indian epistemology stands unique[3] in that it is referred to as the consummation of all knowledge through the progressive removal of the obstructions caused by the sense organs and the mind. As the *Pramāṇa-mīmāṁsa* has it: "The proof of omniscience follows from the proof of the necessity of the final consummation of the progressive development of cognition."[4] Explaining the concept, Mehta writes: "Just as heat is subject to varying degrees and consequently reaches the highest limit, so also cognition which is subject to progressive development owing to the varying degrees of destruction of the obscuring veil, reaches the highest limit, i.e., omniscience when the hindrance of the obscuring *karma* is totally annihilated."[5]

It is interesting to notice here that the discussion of *kevala-jñāna* is found not merely in an epistemological context.[6] The concept figures in a big way also in a discussion of the human ideal to be aimed at. That is, the importance of it from the ethical point of view is also emphasized. It is in this context that the correlation of the theory of *karma* with removing the obstacles to attaining perfect knowledge becomes understandable and it has the effect of identifying the ultimate aim of both epistemology and ethics.

In terms of the Jaina theory of *karma*: omniscience can be attained only after a total destruction of the *mohanīya* (delusion-producing) *karman* followed by a small interval of time and destruction of *jñānāvaraṇa*, *darśanāvaraṇa* and *antarāya* (obstructive) *karmas*. Then it is said that the soul shines in its full splendour and attains omniscience[6] which perceives all substances with all their modes. It is also said that nothing remains unknown in omni-

[2] *Ibid.*, I. 27-30 and the *bhāṣya*

[3] It is unique because in all other schools of Indian philosophy the sense organs and the mind *are not* considered as obstructions in the sense in which Jainism holds them to be obstacles for perfect perception.

[4] I. 1. 16

[5] *Outlines of Jaina Philosophy*, p. 100

[6] The *Nyāyāvatāra*, 28 reads : "The result of the means of knowledge is the removal of ignorance (*ajñāna-nivartanā*); of *kevala-jñāna* bliss and equanimity; and of the rest (other kinds of knowledge) the notion of selecting or rejecting an object (*ādānahāna-dhīḥ*).

[7] See *Tattvārtha-Sūtra*, X. 1 and the *bhāṣya*
See also *Sthānāṅga-Sūtra*, 226

science.[8]

The consummation of all knowledge in *kevala-jñāna* is pointed out by Umāswāmi by referring to a Jaina tradition which holds that when *kevala-jñāna* is attained, the other four types of knowledge, viz., *mati, śruta, avadhi* and *mānaḥparyāya* disappear much in the same way as the other luminous objects in the sky lose their luminosity when the sun appears on the firmament. As can be expected, the thinker supports the traditional view. The argument offered by him is that *kevala-jñāna* is due to the total destruction of the *jñānāvaraṇa karma* whereas the other four are due only to the destruction-cum-subsidence of the *jñānāvaraṇa karma.* Total destruction, he points out, has the possibility of destruction-cum-subsidence.[9]

The uniqueness of the *kevala-jñāna* concept is understandable from the Jaina view that the human soul has the potentiality to know all things, irrespective even of spatial and temporal distance. The potentiality here does not refer merely to man's 'progressive possibility' of purifying his emotions and the will and of acquiring supreme wisdom. The potentiality is pointed to as the human ability to acquire knowledge without the aid at all of the sense organs and the mind. The sense organs and the mind are considered as positive obstructions on the path of acquiring knowledge and hence the ethical disciplines to which man is to subject himself and the control of the senses and the mind will ultimately have to result in the source of obstruction,—the senses and the mind—being removed. The soul's capacity to acquire direct knowledge is subjected to limitations by the *jñānāvaraṇa karma.*

Referring to the potentiality to acquire unlimited knowledge signifies that obstructions to knowledge are not complete, for if they are complete there will not be any difference between the soul (*jīva*) and the not-soul (*ajīva*). This limited capacity necessarily gives us the impression that the sense organs and the mind aid the process of getting knowledge. The sense-object contact through which limited knowledge is acquired is considered wrongly to give us an insight into the 'technique' of knowledge itself. It is not realized that the mistaken notion itself is due to the evil influence of *karma*

8 See *Tattvārtha-Sūtra*, I. 30 and the *bhāṣya*
See also *Āvaśyakaniryukti*, 77

9 See *Tattvārtha-Sūtra bhāṣya*, I. 30

10 *Ibid.*, I. 31

which affects the purity and the capacity of the soul. The realization, on the part of man, that the kārmic particles are the real source of the obstacles to complete knowledge is the first step towards acquiring *kevala-jñāna*; and by undergoing the prescribed course of ethical discipline, the potentiality of the human soul can be fully actualized and man's ultimate goal in life can be reached.

The doctrine being entirely different from that propounded in the other schools it is not surprising to find fundamental objections being raised against the concept itself. The objections by the Mīmāṁsakas are of a fundamental nature and hence we shall consider them and the answers offered to them by the Jainas.

The Mīmāṁsakas, in the first place point out that none of the *pramāṇās* are capable of giving us omniscience or a knowledge of it even. The six sources of knowledge accepted in the Mīmāṁsa system, viz., *pratyakṣa*, *anumāna*, *upamāna*, *āgama*, *arthāpatti* (necessary implication) and *anupalabdhi* (non-comprehension) are pointed out as being ineffective in the matter of giving us knowledge about ominiscience.

The range of perception (*pratyakṣa*) is so limited that in regard to 'the others' whom we perceive we are at the most able to get an idea of the complexion and shape of their bodies and not any idea of even the limited knowledge that they have. It is obvious from this that the perception of the unlimited number of ideas in the mind of the omniscient being is an impossibility according to the Mīmāṁsakas. This is especially so when it is pointed out by the Jainas that the omniscient possesses knowledge of the past, present and the future.

The Jaina's reply is that perception is either transcendental or empirical, the transcendental being divisible into the incomplete and the complete and the empirical being classified into the sensuous and the non-sensuous. In the first case incomplete transcendental knowledge like *avadhi* and *manaḥparyāya* by themselves do not preclude the possibility of omniscience since they deal with things which have form and subtle matter respectively. On the other hand they show us the possibility of perfection in the process of getting knowledge. The non-sensuous refers to intrenal perception like awareness of pleasurable and painful experiences and these by themselves do not disprove the possibility of omniscience.

If it is maintained that sensuous perception disproves the possibility of omniscience, the question would be whose sensuous perception it is—whether it is the enquirer's or that of somebody else. If it is of the enquirer, either it means perception of the moment the doubt about omniscience is expressed or perception relating to all times and places. The first alternative is not contended by the Jaina inasmuch as it stands for the presence of the non-omniscient being. In regard to the second alternative, the statement is made either after experiencing the past, present and the future or without such an experience. The first alternative means that the person who opposes omniscience is himself omniscient and the second alternative points to his dogmatism.

If it is maintained that it is the perception of the others that is responsible for disbelief in omniscience, the argument is still invalid because in that case experience of an 'other' person relating to omniscience, it may just as well be taken to be true. So *pratyakṣa* does not preclude the possibility of omniscience altogether.

The Mīmāṁsaka points out that knowledge of an omniscient person through *anumāna* (inference) is also not possible because the presence of an important requirement of inference, viz., the *hetu* cannot be admitted in the context. Since inference is arrived at by the unconditional, invariable relation between the *hetu* (ground) and the *sādhya* (proven), and since *hetu* which is invariably present along with the *sādhya*,—in this case omniscience—cannot be found, omniscience cannot be known at all. Added to this is the difficulty that omniscience cannot be perceived through the sense organs.

The Jaina reply to this is that if experience of omniscience is pointed out to be impossible, to get a *hetu* which may be negatively connected with omniscience is also impossible. As such the very act of denying the existence of omniscience confirms its presence.

Upamāna or analogy is also ruled out by the Mimāṁsaka to be of any value in our context. Since the emphasis in *upamāna* is on the knowledge about the essential similarities between the objects compared, and since such a thing is not possible in regard to the omniscient being, this source of knowledge also cannot be useful. The Mīmāṁsaka seems to imply that since no one has seen an omniscient person it is all the more difficult to identify any aspect of similarity between him and another who resembles him.

The Jainas meet this objection by pointing out that the most significant point about analogy is that it deals with similarity between things. In virtue of this it is not justifiable to maintain that omniscience itself is impossible.

In regard to *āgama* (authority) the Mīmāṁsaka's position is that only those portions of the Veda which deal with prescriptions and prohibitions are authoritative and in these no mention of an omniscient person is ever made and so omniscience cannot be accepted.

The Jaina's rebuttal of this argument consists in attacking the very concept of an impersonal of *apauruṣeya* scripture considered as authoritative. As there can be only man-made scriptures, and those require omniscient persons to be their authors, in order to be 'authoritative', the possibility of omniscient persons is to be admitted.

The argument by *arthāpatti* (necessary implication) is again not conclusive in the case of the omniscient, says the Mīmāṁsaka. Though the argument in the form in which it is understood in the Mīmāṁsaka system will seek to prove omniscience, the Mīmāṁsakas argue that a teacher need not necessarily be omniscient. This has logically to be their position because they accept only the Veda as the treasure-house of knowledge.

The Jaina here again points out that the significance of *arthāpatti* arises from the fact that it is able to explain a phenomenon, when all other sources of knowledge have failed. The omniscient being is infereable, and so he does not need the help of *arthāpatti*.

Anupalabdhi (non-comprehension) as a *pramāṇa* is again pointed out by the Mīmāṁsa philosophers as not establishing omniscience. The line of argument is that we perceive non-existence only when that which exists is absent. In the case of the omniscient, however, we have not perceived them. We have perceived only the inomniscient and we find them everywhere; so an omniscient person cannot be found at all.

The Jaina reply is that since inference positively proves the existence of the omniscient it is impossible for a *pramāṇa* like *abhāva* to disprove the existence of the omniscient being.

The Mīmāṁsaka relentlessly poses different alternatives and points out that none of the alternatives is feasible. He points out that the term perfect knowledge may mean either a knowledge about all objects or about some principal objects. If the first alternative is accepted, the further question arises whether the 'perception of all objects' is successive or simultaneous. If the perception is successive, it is not true, for successive perception of all things implies the perception of all the objects of the past, present and the future.

When from our common experience we know it is extremely difficult to perceive all the objects of the present how can it be accepted that knowledge of all the objects of the past and the future in addition to those of the present will be possible ? The Jaina's reply is that in *kevala-jñāna* all objects are perceived simultaneously and not successively.

The Mīmāṁsaka's objection against simultaneous perception of different objects is that it is just impossible. "How can", for example, "heat and cold be simultaneously perceived?" he asks. The Jaina points to the fact that in lightning we are able to perceive light as well as darkness simultaneously as evidence to his important contention.

Another point that the Mīmāṁsaka makes is that even granting that 'perception of all' is possible, the individual will become unconscious soon after the complete perception and will then have nothing else to cognize. The Jaina's answer is that the essential feature of omniscience is that there is not a single point of time when there is no cognition, there is no destruction to the cognition, nor to the world. So the objection that the perfect man will become unconscious is invalid.

The Mīmāṁsaka also points out that 'all knowledge' necessarily implies also a knowledge of all desires and so the perfected man himself is likely to be tainted by the desires and he gets obstructions to cognition and his claim to omniscience can no longer be upheld. The Jaina points to the fallacy in the argument. Knowledge of all desires is not the same thing as getting tainted by them. The perfect man is so called because he is able to remain untainted by desires. Moreover, since the sense organs and the mind are responsible for attachments, when the sense organs and the mind are destroyed there is no question of the omniscient person developing attachments.

The final major objection of the Mīmāṁsaka to *kevala-jñāna* is that since the future and the past are non-existent, if they are considered as present in the perfected man it will lead to an illusion proper and so there can't be perfection at all. The Jaina meets the objection by pointing out that the most distinctive feature of the perfected man perceiving the past and the future is that the past is perceived as past and the future is perceived as future. So there is no case of illusion at all here.

The consideration of the various objections to *kevala-jñāna* points to the basic principle behind the concept, viz., that the way of all progress lies in consummation and the process of getting knowledge itself cannot be an exception.

12

Inference

INFERENCE, even as the common man understands it, gives us knowledge 'indirectly.' From the evidences actually presented to man's senses and with the general stock of knowledge he already possesses, he is able to pass from the known to the unknown. The passage from the known to the unknown introduces him to new knowledge and enables him to extend his domain of knowledge. But the whole process is governed by certain principles which ensure a consistent and cogent method by which valid inferences are made.

Paradoxical it may seem but true it is that in spite of the diametrically opposite standpoints that the Jaina system and the traditional Hindu systems take on the question of preception, in regard to the nature of inference they hold the same view. The fundamental Jaina view (traditional) is that what is perceived through the senses is indirect (*parokṣa*) and that which is perceived without the medium of the senses is direct (*pratyakṣa*). In this sense *mati-jñāna* is comprehensive enough to cover inferential knowledge. *Mati-jñāna* proper is considered to pertain to the objects of the senses and is either perceptual or reflective,—the latter covering knowledge by inference. In the traditional Hindu systems since knowledge presented to the senses is considered direct, perceptual knowledge alone is described as direct and inference which is only *based on* perception is regarded as giving us indirect knowledge.

Jainism considers inference to be of two kinds: inference for oneself (*svārthānumāna*) and inference for another (*parārthānumāna*).

The former is referred to as subjective inference and the latter as syllogistic inference. This is clear from the *Nyāyāvatāra* which points out: "Direct knowledge and Inference are sources of both knowledge for oneself and for others. Like the acts of direct cognition and inference, the statements which express them are also called by those names, for, they are means of communication to the others."[1] The latter verses cited are especially significant in our context inasmuch as they unambiguously state that the propositional forms, constituting together an argument, deserve reference as inference. The implication of the verses is that there is accorded full recognition to the syllogistic forms of inference — both the *categorical* and the *hypothetical* — in Jainism.

That inference is considered as a categorical syllogism is evident from the definition: "Inference is that knowledge which determines the major term (*sādhya-niścayaka*) through a mark (*liṅga*) — the middle term — which is invariably connected with the major term."[2] A simpler definition is also found : "Inference is the knowledge of the major term (*sādhya*) by means of the middle term (*sādhana*)."[3]

That inference is considered as a hypothetical syllogism is evident from the definition: "Inference is the knowledge of pervasion (*vyāptijñānaṁ*) based on the presence or absence (of one thing in relation to another), and takes the form : 'If this is, that is ; If that is not, this is not; as for example, If there is smoke there is fire, If there is no fire, there is no smoke."[4]

Subjective inference consists in the knowledge of the probandum from the probans ascertained by one's own self, as having the sole and solitary characteristic of standing in necessary concomitance with the probandum.[5] The term necessary concomitance signifies that in the absence of the one the other also will be absent. The definite cognition of the probans by the individual himself together with his previous knowledge of the invariable concomitance of the probans and the probandum gives him new knowledge and this is subjective inference.

Syllogistic inference comes under *parārthānumāna*. "Syllogistic

1 *Nyāyāvatāra*, 10-13
2 *Ibid.*, 5
3 *Parīkṣāmukha-Sūtra*, III. 9
4 *Ibid.*, 7-8
5 See M. L. Mehta, *Outlines of Jaina Philosophy*, pp. 108-109

inference is definite cognition resulting from a statement of a probans having the characteristic of necessary concomitance with the probandum."[6] The essential Jaina view of the parts of the syllogism is contained in the following words : "The thesis and reason constitute a syllogism adequate for a knowledgeable person."[7] The Jaina view seems to be that the most characteristic feature of an inferential type of knowledge is that the 'reason' being inseparably connected with the probandum, on perceiving the reason, the existence of the probandum is *inferred.* In the classic example, smoke being invariably connected with fire in our everyday experience, on seeing (perceiving) smoke, the inference drawn is the presence of fire. When it comes to listening to a statement, when the proposition that there is smoke on the hill is put forward, the listener jumps to the conclusion (the inference) that the hill has fire. So, strictly speaking only the two propositions :

"The hill is firey" (*pratijñā*) and
"because of smoke" (*hetu*)

make the very inferential process possible. The other three members of the five-membered syllogism are :

"Wherever there is smoke there is fire, such as the kitchen" (*dṛṣṭānta*)
"This hill is smoky" (*upanaya*) and
"therefore it is firey" (*nigamana*)

are, as such, not considered essential or germane to the argument. It is now evident how significant the words "adequate for a knowledgeable person" (in the verse quoted above) are, for they clearly point to the reason why, even in the Jaina tradition, there was a mention of the 5-membered and 10-membered syllogisms. As the Jaina tradition has it: "The syllogism is said to consist of five parts or of ten parts in the alternative. We denounce neither but accept both as legitimate."[8]

The *Pramāṇa-mīmāṁsa* contains definitions of the five members of the syllogism :

"Thesis is the statement of the theme to be proved."[9]

"Statement of a probans ending in an inflexion (*vibhakti*) un-

[6] *Pramāṇa-mīmāṁsa,* II. 1. 1
[7] *Ibid.,* II. 1. 9
[8] *Daśavaikālika-niryukti,* 50
[9] *Pramāṇa-mīmāṁsa,* II. 1. 11

folding the character of probans is called reason."[10]

"Example is the statement of an illustration."[11]

"Application is the act of bringing the probans into connection with the minor term (*dharmin*)."[12]

"Conclusion is the predication of the probandum."[13]

We may, in this connection point out that the second member is considered important since it gives us a hint regarding the conclusion. We may also note that the example may be of two kinds : homogeneous example (*sādharmya dṛṣṭānta*) and heterogeneous example (*vaidharmya dṛṣṭānta*) as is clear from the propositions : "Where there is smoke there is fire" and "Wherever there is no fire, there is no smoke."

The five-membered and the ten-membered syllogisms are accepted in Jainism since they are useful to the layman who is not expected to be an expert in logic. They are also useful while removing a doubt that might have arisen in the mind of the person listening to the argument.

The ten-membered syllogism referred to here is that found in Bhadrabāhu's *Daśavaikālika-niryukti*.[14] The ten members are :

Pratijñā (non-injury to life is the greatest virtue)

Pratijñā-vibhakti (non-injury to life is the greatest virtue according to Jaina scriptures)

Hetu (those who adhere to non-injury are loved by gods and it is meritorious to do them honour)

Hetu-vibhakti (those who do so are the only persons who can live in the highest places of virtue)

Vipakṣa (but even by doing injury one may prosper and even by reviling Jaina scriptures one may attain merit as is the case with brahmins)

Vipakṣa-pratiṣedha (it is not so, it is impossible that those who despise Jaina scriptures should be loved by gods or should deserve honour)

Dṛṣṭānta (the *Arhats* take food from house-holders as they do not like to cook themselves for fear of killing insects)

[10] *Ibid.*, II. 1. 12

[11] *Ibid.*, II. 1. 13

[12] *Pramāṇanayatattvālokaālaṅkāra*, III. 49-50

[13] *Ibid.*, III. 51-52

[14] Cited in S.N. Dasgupta, *op. cit.*, p. 186

Āsaṅkā (but the sins of the house-holders should touch the *arhats*, for they cook for them)

Āsaṅkāpratiṣedha (this cannot be for the *arhats* go to certain houses unexpectedly, so it could not be said that the cooking was undertaken for them)

Naigamana (non-injury is therefore the greatest virtue)

Regarding the ten-membered syllogism Dagupta comments : "These are persuasive statements which are often actually adopted in a discussion, but from a formal point of view many of these are irrelevant."[15] However, it is interesting to note that Dasgupta concedes the earlier origin of the ten-membered syllogism as against the well-known five-membered syllogism of the Nyāya-Vaiśeṣika system when he writes : "When Vātsyāyana in his *Nyāya-Sūtra bhāṣya* I. 1.32 says that Gautama introduced the doctrine of five propositions as against the doctrine of ten propositions as held by other logicians, he probably had this Jaina view in his mind."[16]

[15] *Ibid.*, p. 156
[16] *Ibid.*

PART III
PSYCHOLOGY

13

Mind

THE Jaina view of mind (*manas)* is different from that of the other schools of Indian philosophy as it does not consider mind as one of the sense organs. All the other schools hold the view that mind is also a sense organ. According to Nyāya-Vaiśeṣika pleasure and pain, to be experienced, requires an 'internal organ' (*antaḥkaraṇa*) and that is the mind. A similar status of *antaḥkaraṇa* is accorded to mind by the Mīmāṁsaka system. In regard to the cognition of the self and its attributes it functions independently and in regard to the perception of the objects of the external world it acts in co-operation with the external senses. The basic Sāṁkhya view is the same. It emphasizes the twin-functions of the mind—the sensory and the motor. In this aspect it partakes of the functions of the organs of knowledge (sensory) and organs of conation(motor). In Vedānta also the mind is referred to as an internal organ.

The important point of distinction between Jainism on the one hand and the other schools of Indian philosophy on the other, is accountable from the diametrically opposed views held by them in regard to epistemology. Since the other schools considered knowledge born of the contact of the sense organs with their respective objects to be due to direct perception, knowledge derived through no direct contact between the objects and the senses but whose certainty could none the less be asserted, had to be attributed to the instrumentality of some organ other than the five sense organs *(indriya)*. To be consistent with their own theory they had to conceive of the 'sixth organ' as also of the same kind as the other five sense organs. Hence it was that mind was accorded the status of a sense organ. For instance, experiences of pleasure, pain etc , were direct 'perceptions' but all the same, none of the five sense organs could be considered to have given rise to them. The logical alternative to considering any one of the sense organs as responsible for the perception of pleasure, pain, etc., was to conceive of one other sense organ, and this was mind. Similarly the difficulty regarding transcendental perception *(yogajapratyakṣa)* could be overcome *only* by recognizing an organ other than the five since transcendental perception was something entirely different in nature from that of empirical perception caused by the sense organs.

The Jaina philosophers faced no similar difficulty for accounting for the different type of knowledge that mind is capable of giving, for they considered the knowledge derived through the sense organs as well as the mind to be indirect; they considered the 'instruments' themselves to be positive obstructions to direct knowledge or direct perception. The different modes of deriving knowledge through the mind and the sense organs were to be conceded, all the same, and this resulted in the Jaina conception of the mind as a not-sense (*anīndriya*) and as a quasi-sense (*no-indriya*). In the *Sarvārthasiddhi* it is maintained: "Just as a girl is called *anudara* (without uterus) not because she does not have a uterus but because her womb is so small that it does not possess the capacity of conceiving, so also the mind is called *anīndriya*, since it is not of the rank of ordinary sense organ."[1]

The Jaina philosophers appreciated the fact that there were at least three distinctions between the sense organs and the mind. The sense organs occupy particular sites in the body whereas the mind doesn't. Also the former are 'turned outward' and perceive only the objects external to the perceiver, whereas the latter is 'turned inward' and perceives the internal states and is thus unique in character, and hence referred to as an inner sense (*antaḥ karaṇa*). Furthermore, each of the sense organs has specific objects to perceive and the mind is capable of cognizing all objects of all the sense organs. One reason for this capacity of the mind is that it is subtle. So the mind is also designated as a subtle sense (*sūkṣma-indriya*).

[1] *Sarvārthasiddhi*, I. 14

The distinctions drawn above between the sense organs and mind have been clearly referred to in the *Tattvārtha-Sūtra*[2] and the *Tattvārtha-Sūtra bhāṣya*.[3] Vidyānanda maintains that the reason for considering the mind as unique is the obvious fact that the mind is different from the sense organs. He argues that if mind is regarded as a sense organ because of its instrumentality in getting knowledge even smoke which serves as an instrument of cognition by helping the inferential process should be considered a sense organ.[4] In effect the argument signifies that considering the mind as a sense organ is as absurd as considering the middle term in a syllogistic inference as a sense organ. On the weakness of the argument M.L. Mehta writes: "This argument of Vidyānanda can only refute the position of a psychologist who regards mind as an ordinary sense organ. In the case of smoke the situation is different, since it is not an instrument of the self, being an object of cognition. A sense organ must be an instrument of the self, since the self is the agent that cognizes. Smoke is an ordinary object that can be perceived by the external senses. Hence the status of mind is not like that of an ordinary external sense organ, nor can it be regarded as an object of the senses like smoke. It is the internal instrument that helps the self in cognizing internal states like pleasure, pain, etc."[5]

The most consistent definition of mind is given by Hemacandra who defines mind as the organ of cognition of all objects of all the senses.[6] If the definition were simply that the mind is the one which cognizes all objects, it would not have differentiated the mind from the self since the latter also cognizes all objects. The difference precisely is that the one is dependent on the help of the sense organs whereas the other is not.[7] The *Viśeṣāvaśyaka-bhāṣya* similarly defines *manas* in terms of mental processes.[8] The *Nandi-Sūtra* describes mind as that which grasps everything (*sarvārtha grahaṇaṁ manaḥ*).[9]

[2] *Tattvārtha-Sūtra*, II. 15
[3] *Tattvārtha-Sūtra bhāṣya*, I. 14
[4] *Tattvārtha-śloka-vārttika*, II. 15
[5] *Jaina Psychology*, p. 69
[6] *Pramāṇa-mīmāṁsa*, I. 1. 24
[7] *Ibid.*, Comm.
[8] *Viśeṣāvaśyaka-bhāṣya*, 3525
[9] It is interesting to notice that such an analysis of the mind—defining it in

The definitions are extremely significant in that the self as the agent has been kept out of the list of objects comprehensible by the mind. When perfection is attained, the self, without the help of either the mind or the sense organs, is capable of direct perception and hence it is clear that the mind has its limitation. Its ineffectiveness in aiding perfect perception is, according to the Jainas, the reason why the mind should be considered a positive obstacle to *kevala-jñāna.*

An important implication of the above definitions and commentaries and explanations of the same is that the mind and the self are different from each other. It is in the light of this theory of the distinctness and also limitation of the mind held by the Jaina philosophers that their rejection of the Buddhist theory becomes understandable. A consideration of the Jaina rejection of the Buddhist theory helps us to appreciate the precise nature of the Jaina theory of the mind ; the discussion further points to the distinctness of the self as conceived in Jainism.

The Jaina philosophers, in upholding the existence of an internal organ, the mind, which gives meaning, continuity and coherence to all the 'internal experiences' were naturally critical of the *Vijñānavāda* of the Buddhists which maintained that the various momentary experiences form a connected series by themselves.[10] The Jaina commentator Akalaṅka, for example points out that if the function of *manas* is to consist, as it admittedly does — in judging the comparative goodness or badness of objects in recollection, etc., it is impossible for it to be identified with the momentary *vijñāna*; for, comparisons and recollections are possible only when an object previously perceived can be held before the mind once more; but this is impossible if we have only the *vijñāna* which is to die as soon as it arises.[11]

It will not be out of place here to point out that the distinc-

terms of its functions — found in Indian thought has its parallel in Western psychology. William Mc Dougall in his *Outlines of Psychology*, p. 36 maintains that we have to build up our description of the mind by gathering all possible facts of human experience and behaviour and by inferring from these the nature and structure of the mind. Furthermore, in the same work (p. 42) he points out that we have to build up by inference from the data of the two orders, facts of behaviour and facts of introspection.

[10] The series is referred to as *vijñāna* or *citta* or mind by the Buddhists.

[11] Cited in H.S. Bhattacharya, *op. cit.*, pp. 241-242

tion that the Jainas have taken pains to make between the mind and self is not agreed to by certain other Indian thinkers (in addition to the Buddhists). They consider the distinction unnecessary on the ground that in contradistinction to the sense organs : (i) the mind as also the self are capable of unlimited range of perception of the outside world (ii) the mind, just as the self does not experience any limitation of its 'occasion for co-operation' by contact with the particular object inasmuch as it underlies all the conscious and perceptive processes.

The Jainas were able to maintain the distinction by considering two types of mind, the physical and the psychical, the *dravya-manas* and the *bhāva-manas*. The former is subtle matter transformed into mind and hence is also referred to as the material mind. The *Viśeṣāvaśyaka-bhāṣya* considers the material mind to be composed of an infinite number of fine and coherent particles of matter meant for the function of the mind. There is also the description of the material mind as a collection of fine particles which are meant for exciting thought-processes due to the *yoga* arising out of the contact of the *jīva* with the body.[12]

The psychical mind stands for the mental functions proper. The Jainas firmly believed that unless the *karmas* responsible for obscuring the self from attaining knowledge were annihilated, no knowledge would be possible. The annihilation of the knowledge-obscuring *karmas* and the consequent preparation for the mind's receptivity is the function referred to as *labdhi*. In addition to this, however, there is required the positive modification of the self into the conscious mental activity. It is obvious, these two represent the two aspects of the mind which cannot too rigidly be distinguished. That these two represent the two reciprocal aspects of one and the same function — if we may characterize the activity of the mind in this way — is clearly brought out by Bhattacharya when he writes : "Internal conscious processes, e.g., comparison, conception, etc. are impossible unless and until the conscious principle, the soul is possessed of *labdhi*, i.e., the power of comparing, conceiving, etc. These internal processes are impossible again, unless and until there is *upayoga*, unless and until, that is to say, there is some subjective effort (attention) to carry on these mental processes."[13]

12 *Viśeṣāvaśyaka-bhāṣya*, 3525
13 See H.S. Bhattacharya, *op. cit.*, pp. 243-244

That the Jaina philosophers did not mechanically distinguish between the mind and the self is also evident from the insistence as referred to above on the modification of the self for a proper discharge of the mental function. The functioning of the mind itself is supposed to differentiate a rational being from the irrational. One of the Jaina classics, *Gommaṭasāra* has it : "It is by the help of the *manas* that one can learn, understand the gestures, receive instructions and follow conversation. . .It is through *manas* that one is enabled to decide before doing what ought to be done and what ought not to be done. It is through *manas* that one can learn the distinction between the real and the unreal. It is because one has *manas* that he responds when he is called by his name."[14]

While concluding it is to be noted that the material constituent of the mind, described as *paudgālika*, compounded of peculiar material molecules (*mano-vargaṇa*) is permanent whereas the modifications of it, the modes which are responsible for the mental functions, are not so. But, whatever might be the importance accorded to the grouping of atoms to form the physical mind the conscious activities themselves, it is to be noted that the Jainas strongly believed that in perfection there is no trace of the mental activities, nor of the sensory perceptions.

[14] *Gommaṭasāra, jīva-kāṇda*, 662

14

Sensation and Perception

WHILE translating some of the Saṁskrit terms into English or while comparing certain parallel concepts in other Western systems, sometimes subtle but significant distinctions discernible between terms (within the system under consideration) are lost sight of. The views of some thinkers within the system itself are sometimes mainly responsible for such a confusion regarding fundamental precepts. The Jaina concepts of sensation and perception clearly indicate the pit-falls inherent in an improper analysis of concepts. The scholarly world has been misled into a hasty attempt to mechanically compare Indian with Western concepts.

While distinguishing between *darśana* and *jñāna* we were using, as their English equivalents, the terms *apprehension* and *comprehension* respectively. The epistemological distinction we have drawn has impressed us with the psychological insight of the Jaina philosophers in regard to building up a consistent theory of knowledge. No wonder, therefore, oftentimes we find a comparison being made between *darśana* and sensation on the one hand and *jñāna* and perception on the other. The two stages in the evolution of knowledge, *darśana* and *jñāna* are, in brief, identified as the two psychological stages of sensation and perception. Such a comparison itself is not wrong provided its limitations are borne in mind.

One reason why sensation and *darśana* are mistaken to be identical is that both connote a stage of development from the merely organic state in the evolution of self-consciouness. The Jaina theory of consciousness should not be mistaken to overlook the important fact of development of self-consciousness. The theory of 'continuity of consciousness' signifies also that there are the dormant as well as fully awakened stages of consciousness, the former connoting the stage when there is not even an awareness and the latter indicating the advanced stage in the self-reflective phase in the development of consciousness. The stage of sensation and *darśana* signify that the passive stage of consciousness has been crossed and the stage of sensitivity has been reached.

That the two are different is evident from the logic of the development of consciousness itself. In the Jaina terminology, 'mere awareness of existence' (*sattāmātra*) is clearly a stage antecedent to the stage of becoming aware of the various types of sensation. No doubt, this stage, like the previous one is also indeterminate and stands in clear contrast to the determinate stage of perception or *jñāna* which is to follow. Yet the difference between mere awareness and awareness of sensation though subtle is extremely significant.

We find, even within the Jaina tradition a few philosophers who do not distinguish clearly between sensation and apprehension. A consideration of their views helps us to understand the limitations under which alone a comparison between *darśana* and *jñāna* on the one hand and sensation and perception on the other can be validly made.

Umāswāmi refers to sensation as the implicit awareness of their respective objects by the sense organs.[1] Similarly in the *Āvaśyaka-niryukti* sensation is defined as the awareness of sense data. The specific characteristics of the objects are not noted.[2] Simple awareness of the existence of the object constitutes sensation, according to the views just noted.

That the view has ignored the distinction between sensation and apprehension becomes evident when we analyse it in terms of apprehension and comprehension. We have no doubt maintained that apprehension is indeterminate and comprehension is determinate, but to equate sensation with apprehension would be tantamount to maintaining that apprehension is a category of comprehension. Siddhasena, for instance, maintains that the same cognition is named apprehension in the preliminary stage. The prelimi-

[1] *Tattvārtha-Sūtra*, I. 15
[2] *Āvaśyakaniryukti*, 3

nary stage is nothing but sensation.[3] The difficulty in this position is that apprehension is indeterminate and it is improper to consider it as a category of comprehension which is determinate.[4]

The contradiction involved in considering apprehension itself as sensation is got over by distinguishing three stages through which perception proper is arrived at. The first stage is that of apprehension, the second is that of sensation and the third is that of comprehension. Sensation, according to this view is a stage preceding perception, no doubt, but one which follows apprehension. The idea is expressed in different ways by the different Jaina philosophers, representing this school of thought.

Pūjyapāda says: "On the contact of the object and the sense organs, there occurs apprehension. The cognition of the object thereafter is sensation, as for example the cognition 'this is white colour' (by the visual organ)."[5] It is clearly implied that sensation is different from apprehension or *darśana.* Akalaṅka makes a similar distinction. He maintains: "Sensation is a determinate cognition of the distinctive nature of an object following the apprehension of pure existence emerging just after the contact of a sense organ with its object."[6] Similarly Vidyānanda defines sensation as "the cognition of the specific characters of an object that follows the apprehension of the object in general born of the contact of the sense organ with it."[7] These philosophers thus maintain that the first stage in the complex process of perception is apprehension in which there is mere awareness which is the immediate result of the sense-object contact. In the second stage of sensation, there is some cognition of the specific characteristics of the object. In the third stage, the perception stage (comprehension stage) there is also the 'identification' of the object, for example, as belonging to a particular class, etc. Sensation is thus logically considered to be a category of comprehension, both being conceived of as determinate in nature.

The distinction between apprehension and comprehension and the inclusion of sensation in comprehension is referred to by Vādi-

[3] See *Sanmatitarkaprakaraṇa*, II. 21
[4] See M.L. Mehta, *Jaina Psychology*, p. 74
[5] *Sarvārthasiddhi*, I. 15
[6] See M.L. Mehta, *Jaina Psychology*, p. 75
[7] *Tattvārtha-śloka-vārttika*, I. 15. 2

deva as a distinction between the primary generality of existence (*sattā*) and secondary generality which is less comprehensive in extent. In apprehension alone there is the awareness of the primary generality of existence. In sensation and perception there is only the cognition of a secondary generality. Perception is the consummation of the process commenced in sensation. Vādideva observes: "Sensation is the first stage of comprehension of an object determined by a secondary common feature born of the apprehension that follows the contact of the sense organ with the object, and has mere existence as its object."[8]

The Jaina tradition refers to sensation as being of four kinds : visual, non-visual, clairvoyant and pure.[9] Visual sensation refers to the fact that there is the consciousness of the eyes being affected. Non-visual sensation refers to the 'affection' of the other sense organs, viz., ear, nose, tongue and skin. The clairvoyant sensation, as the name itself indicates, points to the possibility of sense-awareness without the aid of any of the sense organs or even the mind. The last type of sensation refers to the ability of man to have sensation of *all* things in the universe.

Perception (*jñāna*) being a more advanced stage in the development of consciousness is also more complicated. Eight kinds of perception are recognized in Jainism: *ābhinibodhika* or *mati*, *śruta*, *avadhi*, *manaḥparyāya*, *kevala*, *kumati*, *kuśruta* and *vibhaṅga*.[10] The last three are fallacious forms respectively of *mati*, *śruta* and *avadhi*, and so strictly speaking they are not important while considering the psychology of perception.

That perception is a distinct stage of development of consciousness, that it is, though based on sensation, far more complicated than it, is clear from a consideration of the three kinds of *mati-jñāna* found discussed in the Jaina tradition. These are : *upalabdhi* (perception), *bhāvana* (memory) and *upayoga* (advanced understanding).[11] Sometimes we find mention being made of five kinds of *mati-jñāna*. Though the term 'kinds of *mati-jñāna*' is used, it is significant that after they are mentioned it is stated that they are all one, indicating clearly that they refer to the various aspects which go to constitute

8 *Pramāṇanayatattvālokālaṅkāra*, II. 7

9 *Pañcāstikāya, samayaśāra*, 48 ; *Dravya-saṅgraha*, 4

10 *Pañcāstikāya, samayasāra*, 41 ; *Dravya-saṅgraha*, 5

11 *Pañcāstikāya, samayasāra*, 42

mati-jñāna. For example the *Tattvārtha-Sūtra* points out : "*mati* or perception, *smṛti* or memory, *saṁjñā* or conception, *cintā* or induction and *abhinibodha* or deduction are essentially one."[12]

It is because of these various constituents that perception as a psychological process is complicated. In regard to the three-fold aspects of perception referred to above : though the terms 'perception', 'memory' and 'understanding' have definitely different connotations, without the latter two perception itself will not be possible, and, as such they can be considered to have contributed to its very structure. A similar view-point can be maintained in regard to the five-fold aspect of perception. Furthermore, both the types of analysis go to show that perception is dependent not merely on the functioning of the sense organs but also on the mind. This is clearly stated in the *Tattvārtha-Sūtra* which maintains that perception is dependent on either the sense organs or the mind. The former is referred to as *indriya-nimitta-mati-jñāna* and the latter, as *anīndriya-nimitta-mati-jñāna.*[13] In the light of the analysis of the various aspects of perception given above, the view that "the Jaina psychologists are far from maintaining that a fully developed perception is a simple psychosis"[14] can be accepted as clearly reflecting the Jaina theory of perception.

Thus it is clear that the Jaina psychology of sensation and perception is not gathered fully from the concepts of *darśana* and *jñāna.* The parallellism between *darśana* and *jñāna* on the one hand and sensation and perception on the other can be emphasized, but not without noting the limitations involved.

[12] *Tattvārtha-Sūtra,* I. 10
[13] *Ibid.,* I. 14
[14] H.S. Bhattacharya, *op. cit.,* p. 299

15

Emotions and Feelings

THE philosophic significance of analysing emotions and feelings consists in its suggesting to man ways and means of evolving himself to become the true human *person* that he essentially is. We may describe the aim of the psychological analysis as consisting in its catering to the innate need for a total integration of the human personality. Taking man as he *is* rather than what he *ought* to be, philosophers have referred to the different aspects of the human mind and especially to the dangers which accompany their lop-sided development. It is in the light of this that the Indian philosophers' repeated emphasis on mind-control becomes explicable. The classic way in which man is exhorted to attain personality-integration that we find in Indian thought has been to suggest to him that if he were to attain the ultimate end in life (variously described by Indian philosophers – both orthodox and heterodox) he has to 'look within' and rid himself of all the impurities that his soul is subjected to.

The aim of life, having been posited by the Jaina philosophers as regaining the pristine purity of consciousness we find them emphasizing the necessity to free the *jīva* from the *ajīva*. Since the particles of *karma* are directly responsible for the *jīva-ajīva* contact, purifying consciousness of its sloth ultimately consists in stopping the inflow of *karma*.

The Jaina theory of emotions and feelings is clearly discernible in the phenomenological analysis it gives of *jīva*. Though from a transcendental standpoint *jīva* is nothing but pure consciousness, from the empirical point of view it is seen to be possessed of passions (*kaṣāyas*) due to the influence of nescience (*avidya*) which is as much beginningless as the *jīva* itself. Both *jīva* and *avidya* being beginningless, it is not easy to say when the *jīva* came in contact with *avidya*. In fact their contact is also beginningless.[1] The passions are helped by what is known as *yoga*, vibrations of body, speech and mind. The *Tattvārtha-Sūtra* points to these two, viz., *kaṣāyas* and *yoga* as the main causes of bondage.[2] It is now evident how closely the analysis of emotions and feelings are related to the Jaina analysis of the purpose of human existence.

Analysis of feeling is easier since it can be explained in terms of bodily sensations than an analysis of emotion which relates to the mind. In the Jaina terminology *vedanīya-karma* is responsible for sense feeling and *mohanīya-karma* or delusion-producing *karma* is responsible for emotions.

The Jaina philosophers point out that at the basis of all feeling is the element of passion because of which we have the pleasant and the unpleasant sensations. That is, the Jaina maintains a subjectivist point of view in regard to pleasure and pain. There is nothing which is considered as pleasure by all, nor as pain by everyone. The *Uttarādhyayana-Sūtra* maintains that it is the passionate man who feels the bodily and mental sensations of pleasure and pain.[3] Neither indifference nor emotion is the direct outcome of pleasure. It is because of love and hate that man experiences pleasure and pain. No one object in the world has the power to cause any feeling — pleasurable or painful — to a man who is determined to be indifferent towards them.

A positive illustration of the state of non-attachment towards pleasure and pain that the Jaina posits as the end of human life is found in his concept of the omniscient (*kevala-jñānin*). Our reference earlier (though in an epistemological context) to the Jaina view regarding the obstructive role that the sense organs and the mind play in human life has already indicated that the state of perfection (which is also synonymous with omniscience) is characterized by man's remaining unaffected by pleasure and pain. The *Tattvārtha-Sūtra* refers to the omniscient as one who is free from

1 U. Misra, *op. cit.*, p. 262
2 *Tattvārtha-Sūtra,* VIII. 1
3 *Uttarādhyayana-Sūtra, XXXII.* 100-106

all liking (*rati*) and disliking (*arati*).[4] It logically follows that he does not have either the feeling of pleasure or the feeling of pain. Since *by hypothesis* the omniscient person has freed himself of the limitations imposed on him, preventing him from experiencing pure bliss, it is obvious, he is also beyond 'pleasure' and 'pain' which have their roots in the senses and the mind.

Here an interesting question arises. If pleasure and pain are pure subjective experiences, does the external world have no role to play in the production of feelings? Though the Jaina maintains emphatically that the external world is not the causal factor, he does not swing to the other extreme of maintaining that it does not have any role whatever. He attributes the feelings to *karma* rather than to *ajīva*. According to him the feeling-producing *karma* is responsible for the emergence of the feelings of pleasure and pain. The *sata-vedanīya-karma* is responsible for the feeling of pleasure and the *asata-vedanīya karma* is responsible for the feeling of pain. The external world is thus the helping cause in reaping the fruit of the feeling-producing *karma*. It is the medium through which and which alone man suffers or enjoys. In the absence of the rise of the corresponding *karma*, an external object alone is not considered to be competent enough to give rise to the feeling of pleasure or pain.[5]

The conditional role that the world of objects plays in the production of feeling thus becomes apparent. The object in question (whether it is the causal factor) is thus not the essential but only a helping cause. For, as Mehta points out, if it is not admitted, a thing which is pleasurable in one's case would be pleasurable to others as well. The same thing holds good in regard to painful things. Besides, different sensations may produce the same feeling and the same sensation may give rise to different feelings in different moods.[6]

The upshot of the Jaina analysis is that man is not inevitably and irretrievably subjected to feelings of pleasure and pain; that he can, by exercising his will, attain a stage where he remains unaffected by either; that when such a stage is reached he has realized personality-integration.

4 *Tattvārtha-Sūtra*, X. 1
5 M.L. Mehta, *Jaina Psychology*, p. 115
6 *Ibid*, pp. 115-116

Emotion is more complicated in nature and hence we find different types of emotions described. The main analysis that we find of the concept (psychological fact) is in terms of *karma*. One of the eight types of *karma* — *mohanīya karma* is considered responsible for the rise of human emotions. The sub-division of *mohanīya karma* into the *darśanāvaraṇa* and *cāritra mohanīya* (right conduct-deluding) *karmas* is indicative of the psycho-ethical characteristic of the Jaina theory of emotions. As Mehta points out : ". . . the Jaina conception of emotion is not purely psychological. It is psycho-ethical in character. We are not in a position to separate the two, since the conception is fundamentally based on the theory of conduct."[7]

The two types of delusion-producing *karmas* referred to above give us an insight into the essentially philosophic application of the theory of emotions that we find in Jainism. The first of the two types is a result of obstruction of right vision. The corollary of this is that right conduct is made impossible. It is familiar to everyone that unless the individual has spiritual conviction there is not even a possibility of his treading the right path. The *Gommaṭasāra* points to emotion as having the power to debar the self from having spiritual conversion, partial conduct, complete conduct and perfect conduct."[8]

We find four types of emotions being mentioned in the Jaina classics. These are anger (*krodha*), pride (*mana*), deceit (*māya*) and greed (*lobha*). Each one of them is again considered to be classifiable into four, so that we have in all sixteen types of emotions enumerated. Each emotion is of the following four kinds : (i) *anantānubandhi*, i.e., that which obscures spiritual conversion; (ii) *apratyākhyānāvaraṇa*, i.e., that which eclipses the proneness to partial conduct; (iii) *pratyākhyānāvaraṇa passion*, i.e., that which arrests the aptitude for complete conduct; and (iv) *saṁjvalana*, i.e., that which baulks the perfect type of conduct, thus thwarting the attainment of arhatship.[9]

In addition to the above, nine milder emotions are also described. These are : laughter (*hāsya*), love (*rati*), hatred (*arati*), grief (*śoka*), fear (*bhaya*), disgust (*juguspa*), hankering after man

[7] *Ibid.*, p. 122
[8] *Gommaṭasāra*, 282
[9] *Sarvārthasiddhi*, VIII. 9

(*puruṣaveda*), hankering after woman (*strīveda*) and hankering after both the sexes (*napuṁsakaveda*).[10]

Emotional disturbance in man results in acts of various kinds which in turn entangle him more and more into the shackles of life's varied experience. In terms of Indian thought involvement in life characterized by emotions and passions prevents man from escaping from the cycle of birth and death. Since emotions differ in intensity, actions resulting from them have also differing effects on the individual *jīva* by determining the 'period of bondage'. The Jaina philosophers make use of the term *leśya* to indicate the closely-knit pattern resulting from the mingling of passion and action. Activity coloured by passions is described as *leśya*.[11] We need not go into all the details about the various types of *leśya*, but suffice it to make note of the fact that passions in general excite the senses to indulge themselves in sensuous objects. K.C. Sogani makes a significant point when he observes that this may itself be considered as a proof for the view that knowledge by the senses is liable to be infected by passions. They work to such an extent that when pleasant things depart and unpleasant ones come closer, one is put to severe anxiety and it results in the loss of mental serenity.[12]

Ultimately speaking, the result of emotional disturbance (which is itself symptomatic of the loss of mental equanimity) is that the *jīva* gets enmeshed in the kārmic cycle more and more. The Jaina theory of emotion is thus consistent with their ethical theory in so far as the latter contains in it the definite suggestion that sensory and mental excitations are ultimately hindrances to man's enjoying purity of bliss and fullness of existence.

[10] *Ibid.*, VIII. 9

[11] *Gommaṭasāra*, 489

[12] K.C. Sogani, *Ethical Doctrines in Jainism* (Sholapur : Jaina Saṁskṛti Saṅgha, 1967), p. 54

16

Extra Sensory Perception

THE phenomenon of perceiving without the help of either the sense organs or the mind which is accepted as a 'fact' by modern psychologists has been speculated about and argued for long time ago by the Indian psychologists. The exceptions were the Cārvākas and the Mīmāṁsakas. The former did not accept the concept of E. S. P. on the principle of not accepting anything not perceived by the sense organs. The latter's reliance on the Vedas was so much that they considered no other source as capable of giving a knowledge of the past, present and the future; naturally the phenomenon of E. S. P. was not considered to be meaningful since it was not derived from the Vedas.

The Jaina view of the E.S.P. is easily understandable from the fact that the sense organs and the mind were considered by the Jaina philosophers to impose limitations on man's capacity to attain full knowledge (*kevala-jñāna*) and from their theory that progressively man could remove the obstructive veils to omniscience to enjoy its full blaze. In man's march towards attaining direct perception two stages, clearly reflecting (though only approximating to) the 'immediate knowledge' are discernible. These are clairvoyance (*avadhi*) and telepathy (*manaḥparyāya*) and offer us an insight into the ultimate potentiality of the human self whose essential nature is consciousness. Let us consider them in some detail.

Clairvoyance (*Avadhi-jñāna*) refers to man's capacity to perceive, without the help of either the sense organs or the mind, things which have shape and form. Perception of formless things such as souls, *dharma*, *adharma*, *space*, and *time* is beyond the scope of clairvoyance. So only those things which have shape, colour and extension can be peceived in clairvoyance.[1]

Different people are considered to possess varying capacities for clairvoyance. The differences are attributable to the fact that the kārmic veils responsible for man's limitations in his capacity for direct perception are not removed by all men simultaneously. Hence men being in the different stages of successfully getting over the limitations imposed on them by their own *karmas*, their capacities also show wide divergences. The lowest capacity for clairvoyance signifies man's capacity to perceive objects possessing the minimum possible space and to penetrate the smallest conceivable point of time. Qualitatively the best type of clairvoyance is the one in which there is the perception of objects occupying an infinite number of space-points and the penetration into countless number of cycles of time, both past and future. It should be noted here that with the increase in capacity for time-penetration, the capacity for space-penetration (and along with it the capacity for comprehending more number of material atoms and more number of modes) also increases but not *vice versa*.[2]

The rationale of the argument, according to Tatia, is this: "A time-point is more extensive as compared with a space-point and so it is held that it is easier to extend over one space-point than to penetrate one time-point. So it is conceived that temporal penetration is necessarily accompanied with spatial extension. But the reverse is not true. As each space-point can contain an infinite number of atoms, and each atom has an infinite number of modes, it is conceived that with the increase of scope in space, there is necessarily an increase in the number of things and their modes that are comprehended, but the comprehension of a greater number of things and modes not necessarily involve more penetration into time and extension in space. Comprehension of a greater number of things and modes may be due to clarity of the intuition as well and this is another reason why it does not necessarily involve spatial or temporal extension."[3]

Even in the best type of clairvoyance, however, not all modes

[1] *Tattvārtha-Sūtra*, 1.28
[2] See *Āvaśyakaniryukti*, 36
[3] See *Studies in Jainism*, p. 64

are known, though the modes known are infinite in number.[4] It is also held that all living beings — not merely human beings — are considered to possess (in varying degrees) the capacity for clairvoyance.

There is a three-fold classification of *Avadhi-jñāna*: the *deśāvadhi*, the *paramāvadhi* and the *sarvāvadhi*. The range of the first type is limited by spatial and temporal conditions, while that of the second type is not so limited. *Sarvāvadhi* is the faculty by which we may perceive the non-sensuous aspects of all the material things of the universe. The *deśāvadhi* is subdivided into two kinds, — the *bhāvapratyaya* or congenital and the *guṇapratyaya* or acquired. The faculty of *deśāvadhi* is connote in the superhuman beings of the heavens and the hells. The acquired modes of the *deśāvadhi* is due to the destruction or subsidence-in-part of the obstacles that hinder the operation of clairvoyance. The *guṇa-pratyaya avadhi* may be acquired by all beings who have the mind. It is considered to be of the following six types: (i) *anugāmi*, the type of clairvoyance which continues to exist even if a person leaves a particular place and goes elsewhere; (ii) *ananugāmi*, the type of clairvoyance which is just the opposite of the previous one; (iii) *vardhamāna*, clairvoyance which increases in its scope and duration as time passes ; (iv) *hīyamāna*, clairvoyance which decreases in its intensity with the passage of time; (v) *avasthitā*, clairvoyance which neither increases nor decreases (in intensity and duration); and (vi) *anavasthitā*, clairvoyance which sometimes increases and sometimes decreases (in scope).[6]

Telepathy (*Manaḥparyāya*) stands for man's capacity to directly apprehend the modes of other minds.[7] The Jaina conception of the mind that it is made of subtle matter offers us an insight into the principle of telepathy. The mind-stuff is considered to reflect in the different modes of the mind. The modes are nothing but the reflections of the different states of thought experienced in the mind. Hence a person possessing telepathy is believed to directly cognize the mental states of others without the instrumentality

4 See *Viśeṣāvaśyka-bhāṣya*, 685 ; *Nandi-Sūtra*, 16

5 See H.S. Bhattacharya, *op. cit.*, pp. 307-08

6 *Nandi-Sūtra*, 9-15 ; *Tattvārtha-Sūtra*, *bhāṣya* on 1. 23

7 *Āvaśyakaniryukti*, 76

of the sense organs and the mind.[8] In contrast to the capacity for clairvoyance, telepathy is limited to human beings. Telepathy is achieveable only after undergoing the prescribed course of rigorous discipline and an arduous process of character-building. The *Nandi Sūtra* lists the conditions under which telepathy occurs in man:[9]

(i) the human beings in the *karma-bhūmi* must have fully developed sense organs and a fully developed personality, i.e., they must be *paryāpta*; (ii) must possess right attitude, *samyagdṛṣṭi*, and as a consequence they must be free from passion; and (iii) must be self-controlled and they must be possessed of extraordinary powers.

In regard to the fundamentals of telepathy the Jaina philosophers are all agreed but in regard to one point there is no unanimity of views. Umāswāmi maintains that the objects perceived by other minds are known directly in telepathy. The process of change undergone by the mind does not stand in the way of the objective contents being intuited directly. Jīnabhadra on the other hand holds the view that the states of the mind-substance are directly intuited but their objective contents are only indirectly perceived. The reason he gives is that the 'contents' of the mind may include material as well as non-material objects. Since it is absurd to think of intuiting the thoughts of others without the medium of the changing states of the mind, it is more logical to hold that the material as well as non-material objects are cognized only indirectly. Probably the earlier (traditional) Jaina conception was that the states (*paryāyas*) of the mind (*manas*) are directly perceivable. The term *manaḥparyāya* was probably literally understood.

Telepathy is considered to be of two kinds: *ṛjumati* and *vipulamati*.[10] The former is considered to represent a lower stage in man's spiritual evolution, and hence as less pure. The latter is considered to last till the dawn of omniscience. *Ṛjumati* is believed to be effective in knowing the thoughts of beings that are situated within the range: four to eight *krośas* to four to eight *yojanas*. The

[8] *Viśeṣāvaśvaka-bhāṣya*, 669, 814

[9] *Nandi-Sūtra*, 39 & 40

[10] The latter is considered to be purer (*viśuddhatara*) than the former ; and while the former might cease (*pratipatati*), the latter cannot. (*na pratipatati*)—*Tattvārtha-Sūtra*, I. 24 & 25

See also *Sthānāṅga-Sūtra*, 72

range of *vipulamati* similarly is : four to eight *yojanas* to two half *dvīpas*. The temporal range of *ṛjumati* is between one life-time to eight past and eight future lives. *Vipulamati's* temporal range is between eight and infinite number of incarnations.

From the description above of clairvoyance and telepathy it will be noted that both of them have reference to material objects. Yet there are some differences between the two. They can well be tabularized as follows :

	CLAIRVOYANCE	*TELEPATHY*
Purity	Perception of material object and even mind is possible but it is not as clear as it is in the case of telepathy.	Perception is more lucid than in clairvoyance. Even other minds are more clearly cognized.
Scope	Infinite degrees are possible. From the perception of the minutest part of space to its limits.	It is limited to the sphere inhabited by the human beings only.
Subject	Possible for all living beings and in all the possible states they exist.	Possible only for man and only after registering some spiritual progress.
Objects	Limited to material objects; not all the infinite number of modes are perceived.	Comparatively telepathy extends to even minutest parts.

17

Self

THE Jaina conception of self is understandable easily from the conception of Substance as identity-and-change. The various mental experiences of man point to something which is the experient, some *constant entity* which gives meaning and significance for the changing modes. This is the soul or the self. The distinguishing feature of the Jaina conception of self from that of the Buddhist view at once becomes apparent. The fact of changing modes is pointed out by the Buddhists to maintain their theory that the 'self' is nothing but a bundle of experiences, whereas the same fact is pointed to by the Jainas to reiterate their view that there must be some constant factor because of which alone the changing modes are recognized as changing.

The essential quality of the self is consciousness. Consciousness is the attribute which distinguishes the living from the non-living and the Jaina has no difficulty in admitting, in principle, that "even the state of deep sleep is not without consciousness, for, if it is not admitted, the pleasant experience of a comfortable and sound sleep recalled in the subsequent waking state would be impossible."[1]

Consciousness presupposes the various aspects of the self and also their corresponding functions. Accordingly we find the soul being described as "the knower (*pramātṛ*), that which illumines itself and others (*svānya-nirbhāsin*), the doer, the enjoyer, the chang-

[1] See M.L. Mehta, *Jaina Psychology*, p. 31

ing (*vivṛttimān*), that which is proved by its own self, consciousness (*sva-samvedana-saṁsiddha*) ; one different in nature from the earth and the other elements."[2] The three aspects of consciousness, viz., the cognitive, affective and conative which are implied in the description of soul made just now, are made explicit in another Jaina classic which makes a distinction between consciousness as knowing, as feeling and as experiencing the fruits of *karma* and willing.[3] A phenomenological description of the soul is also found. "The soul is the Lord (*prabhu*), the doer (*kartā*), enjoyer (*bhoktā*) and limited to his body (*dehamātra*), still incorporeal, and as ordinarily found with *karma*. As a potter considers himself a maker and enjoyer of the clay-pot, so from the practical point of view, the mundane soul is said to be the doer of things like constructing house and the enjoyer of sense objects."[4] It is interesting in this context to find William James distinguishing between the self as known or the *me*, the empirical ego as it is sometimes called and the self as knower or the I, pure ego. He considers the empirical self to consist of the "entire collection of consciousness, the psychic faculties and dispositions taken concretely. But the pure self is considered to be very different from the empirical self. "It is the thinker, that which thinks. This is permanent, what the philosophers call the soul or the transcendental ego."[5]

The Jaina philosophers anticipated an objection to pointing out to consciousness as the distinct phenomenon in the living being, viz., that such a portrayal of the living entity does no justice to so many other characteristics like existence, origination, decay and permanence. In answering the objection they have pointed to the distinction between a definition and a description. The former pin-points the factor of distinction found in the thing defined whereas the latter considers the entity as a whole and analyses its constituents to their minutest detail. . .[6]

The differentiating characteristic of a living being, according to the *Tattvārtha-Sūtra* is its being a substratum of the faculty of cognition (*upayoga*)[7] which is only a manifestation of consciousness in

2 *Nyāyāvatāra*, 31
3 *Pañcāstikāyasāra*, 38
4 *Ibid.*, 27 , *Samayasāra*, 124
5 *Principles of Psychology*, Vol. I, p. 292
6 See *Tattvārtha-Sūtra*, V. 29
7 *Ibid.*, II. 8

a limited form. Apprehension (*nirākāra-upayoga*) and Comprehension (*sākāra-upayoga*), the two types of cognition recognized in Jainism are only imperfect projections of consciousness. Only in perfect apprehension and perfect comprehension consciousness manifests itself fully. The living being's potentiality is not confined to perfect apprehension and perfect comprehension alone ; it extends also to perfect bliss and infinite power. Consciousness in its purity is thus a potentiality to start with and its actualization is the aim of ethical and spiritual life. The purity of consciousness is lost due to the four types of *karma*, – the apprehension-obscuring *karma*, comprehension-obscuring *karma* – deluding *karma* and the power-obscuring *karma*. Since it is accepted by the other schools of Indian philosophy (except the Cārvāka school) that the distinctiveness of the human species consists in the progressive realization of the state of perfection the Jaina view that the self manifests itself only partially in living beings in general is understandable and acceptable.

Though the 'self' or the 'soul' may be considered to be a metaphysical abstraction and requires to be probed into by the metaphysician it is nonetheless the business of the psychologist to examine its nature and assert its existence, for, consciousness is a central concept in psychology and an understanding of it is directly related to the existence of a soul.[8] Also, the ancient Indian philosophers's understanding of the various dimensions of the human personality enabled him to appreciate that analysing the psychical aspects of man need not and should not be considered an end-in-itself. Hence it was considered that the metaphysical and the psychological analyses were not to be carried out as if they were totally unrelated. The Jaina philosophers were no exception to this general approach to man found in Indian thought.

The various psychic phenomena which are the manifestations of consciousness are, in terms of contemporary psychology, 'active states' and these imply the existence of a concrete agent, the self or the soul. The self is non-material since its activities are self-

[8] Cf. James Ward, *Psychological Principles*, p. 370 who refers to 'internal perception' or 'self-consciousness'. "The last order of knowledge of the duality of subject and object is an indispensable condition of all actual experience, however simple. It is therefore first in order of experience. It is the subject of experience that we call the pure ego or self."

determined and spontaneous. Were it to be made of matter, its activities would have been determined from outside and it would not have been capable of immaterial thought-activity. Hence it is held that the 'self' or the 'soul' is both substantial and non-material in nature. It is interesting to note here that the American philosopher, William James, implies that a non-material conception of a 'soul' is not unacceptable. He writes : ". . . to posit a soul influenced in some mysterious way by the brain-states and responding to them by conscious affections of its own, seems to me the line of least logical resistances so far as yet we have attained."[9]

In one of the Jaina classics, *Viśeṣāvaśyaka-bhāṣya* we find the problem of existence or otherwise of the soul being discussed at length. Mahāvīra is portrayed as giving suitable answers to the objections raised by Indrabhūti representing the opposite school of thought which does not accept the existence of soul. As is found in most of the Indian philosophical classics, we find, in the Jaina classic also, the opponents' view-point stated first, and then a systematic refutation of the various arguments put forward in its favour. Lord Mahāvīra himself states the opposite point of view : "The existence of soul is doubtful since it is not directly perceived by any of the sense organs. The case of the soul is not similar to that of the atoms, for, though the latter also are imperceptible, as collectivities they are perceptible. Inference is also of no use in asserting the soul's existence since no inference is possible without some element of perception. On scriptural authority also the existence of the soul cannot be proved since scriptural knowledge is not distinct from inferential knowledge. Even granting that scripture aids our understanding of the existence of the soul, scripture itself does not contain the experiences of anyone who has directly perceived the soul. Added to all these difficulties in regard to scripture is the fact that there are mutual contradictions between scriptural passages. The analogical argument cannot even be attempted to establish the soul's existence, for, there is not a single entity in the universe which bears even remote resemblance to the soul. In the absence of proof through any of the means of valid knowledge considered, the only valid conclusion is that the soul does not exist."[10]

9 *op. cit.*, Vol. I, p. 181

10 *Viśeṣāvaśyaka-bhāṣya*, 1550-53

Mahāvīra's main fort of defence is apparent from his words : "O Indrabhūti ! the self is indeed directly cognizable to you also. Your knowledge about it which consists of doubts, etc., is itself the self. What is proved by your own experience should not be proved by other means of knowledge. No proof is required. . . (for) the existence of happiness, misery, etc." Also "the self is directly experienced owing to *ahaṁpratyaya* — the realization as 'I' in 'I did', 'I do', and 'I shall do', — the realization which is associated with the functions pertaining to all the three terms."[11] That Mahāvīra's maintaining that no proof is required for maintaining the existence of a soul is not a case of evading a reply to a basic question is evident from his specifically stating that the existence of a doubt presupposes a doubter. He asks : "If the object about which one has doubt is certainly non-existent, who has a doubt as to whether I do exist or I do not exist ? Or, Gautama (Indrabhūti !) When you yourself are doubtful about your self, what can be free from doubt ?"[12]

The self-validity of the existence of a thing, Mahāvīra maintains, is evident from the self-evident characteristic of the attributes themselves. He says : "The self which is the substratum of its attributes is self-evident owing to the attributes being self-evident, as is the case with a pitcher. For, on realizing the attributes, the substratum, too, is realized."[13] The self whose attributes are beyond doubt, point to the existence not merely of the attributes but of their substratum as well. The relation that obtains between a substance and its attributes is of the reciprocal type and as such we cannot conceive of either of the relata without reference to the other. For the same reason, from the existence of one of the relata the existence of the other can be inferred.

Moreover, sometimes it is seen that the qualities such as sensation, perception, memory, etc., are absent even when the body is present as in sound sleep, death, etc.[14] From this it is evident that the body is not necessarily related to the mental activities, i.e., there is some substance other than the body and that is the soul.

Lastly, the body which is nothing but material (*pudgala*) cannot

[11] *Ibid.*, 1554-56
[12] *Ibid.*, 1557
[13] *Ibid.*, 1558
[14] See M.L. Mehta, *Jaina Psychology*, p. 38

by itself account for consciousness. If the bodv as a whole does not possess consciousness as an attribute of its various parts, consciousness which *is* found associated with the body must be the characteristic of the soul or the self which associates itself with the body. The soul's association with the body brings consciousness to it and the dissociation of the soul brings about absence of consciousness in the body. These indicate clearly that consciousness is the essential characteristic of the soul or the self.

The Jaina conception of the self is thus understood in terms of consciousness, its essential characteristic. It may also be said that the Jaina idea of consciousness can itself be comprehended by considering the concept of self.

18

Metempsychosis

THE doctrine of immortality of the soul and the consequent belief in reincarnation or rebirth is central to the *karma* theory in Jainism as it is in Hinduism. The six alternatives suggested in the *Sthānāṅga-Sūtra* clearly indicate the immortality of the soul. For a soul enter into another body, i. e., take another birth, may be accounted for in six ways : (1) the bad deeds done during the present life require another life—and this may be the next life itself or a life after that ; (2) the bad deeds done in the last or a previous life may be fructifying during the present life; (3)the bad deeds done, similarly in a previous life might not have fructified till now, and may not bear fruit in the rest of the present life and so may require another life. That is, the fruits for an evil act indulged in a previous life may have to be borne in the next life or in a life after the next. In regard to good deeds similarly : (4) those of the present life may bear fruit in the next life or in some future life ; (5) those of the previous life or of one of the past lives may be having their good effects during the present life ; and (6) the good deeds of either the last life or of one of the past lives might not have yielded their fruits in the present life till now or may not yield the fruits in the rest of the present life, thus requiring another life. Though the fructification may take place in the next life itself there is no guarantee that this will happen.[1]

It may be mentioned here that the possibilities of (1) the good

[1] IV. 2. 7

karmas done during the present life bearing their fruits in the present life itself and (2) the bad *karmas* of a particular life bringing to bear their evil effects in that life itself have also been pointed out, but in the wider context of indicating the way in which one's own actions (good as well as bad) will have to be answered by the individual.[2]

When the immortality and reincarnation of the soul are asserted, an important question arises. Does reincarnation connote always an upward evolution, so that once the stage of the human being is attained, there is no danger of slipping down the scale of evolution to attain a sub-human stage ? Even the common man may probably answer the question in the negative. No doubt, it may be argued that the proviso that a person indulging in evil acts has to undergo suffering for the same and this in itself is a just punishment for the evil-doer. Read along with the implication that such a person naturally encounters the situation of his having to stay on at the human level without any prospects of an upward evolution, it seems that the possibility of man slipping down need not even be thought of. But the strict application of the theory of *karma* requires, the common man may suggest, that if acts indulged in by man do not befit the status and dignity of man but that of a sub-human level, the individual be pushed down the human level. The Jaina view is that a just punishment requires a corresponding degradation even in the level of life.

Mehta, clarifying the Jaina view, refers to the theosophist's view that once consciousness attains to the human level, 'there is no return', that if evil reaches a stage beyond redemption there may be an utter dissolution of that entity and that though man may become a super-man, he will never be less than man and points out that the view is influenced by the theory of evolution and that the Jaina tradition has never entertained this notion of the theosophists. He writes : "The Jaina holds that the soul of a human being after death can go back to animals or vegetables. It may also go to heaven and live there for some time. Thus he believes in the retrogression of the souls. He does not believe in the theory of growth and progress of the souls from lower to higher states of consciousness."[3]

[2] *Ibid*

[3] *Jaina Psychology*, pp. 176-77

In respect of the belief in retrogression of souls, the Jaina view bears a remarkable resemblance with the Hindu view. Various Upaniṣads make references to the possibility of retrogression :

"Those who do not know these two paths become insects, gnats, mosquitoes...."[4]

"Those who possess good conduct here would attain good birth...Those who are of bad conduct here would attain evil birth, the birth of a dog, that of a hog. .."[5]

"Some persons according to their *karma* and inclination of mind take another birth. Some others again are degenerated into the states of trees."[6]

"He is born on this earth as a worm, a grasshopper, a fish, a bird, a lion, a boar, a snake, a tiger or another creature in one or other station according to his deeds."[7]

In this context it is important to bear in mind the four states of being of the *jīva* or the conscious principle, the soul : the state of hell, the animal state, the human state and the heavenly state. The term *jīva* connotes the conscious principle in the universe and this is found not merely in the human being. This gives us the cue to the Jaina theory of reincarnation, since it unambiguously points to the fact that the human stage is only one of the stages in which we find the conscious principle, and as such we do not have any right to imagine that once the human state is attained, attainment of the super-human and the perfection state-connoting the permanent escape from the cycle of birth and death is something automatic. The *Bhagavatī-Sūtra* makes specific references to the four states of the soul and points to the *karmas* which are responsible for entrance into them. The *karma* leading to the bondage of hellish life is the result of possessing immense wealth, indulging in violent deeds, killing the beings of five sense organs, eating flesh, etc. The *karma* leading to the life of animals, vegetables and the like is the consequence of deceiving others, practising fraud, speaking untruth, etc. The *karma* leading to human life is the result of simplicity of behaviour, humble character, kindness, compassion, and so on. The *karma* leading to

4 *Brahadāraṇyaka Upaniṣad*, VI. 2. 16
5 *Chāndogya Upaniṣad*, V. 10. 7
6 *Kaṭhopaniṣad*, II. 2. 7
7 *Kauśitāki-brāhmaṇa*, I. 1. 6

the enjoyment of celestial life is the result of practising austerities, observing vows and the like."[8]

The significant point regarding the Jaina theory of retrogression is that it supplies the basis for an ethics of responsibility. The *karma* theory in general, with its corollary, the theory of reincarnation, even in the popular understanding, provides the basis for an ethic of individual responsibility. In the Jaina theory this principle is accepted but there is an emphatic assertion that if man is a responsible being, he is responsible not merely for the good and bad acts he does at the human level and for which he answers at the human level,—in the same or in a future life. If his sense of responsibility is really to play the significant role in the matter of perfecting himself by elevating him far above the ordinary human level, it cannot but be brought in when he errs, when he commits acts which have the mark of the animal in them. He cannot indulge in acts which are beneath his dignity as a human being and escape the consequences. He gets degraded and is pushed down to the sub-human level.

Another factor which helps us to understand the Jaina theory in its proper perspective is that whenever we discuss man and his efforts to realize his ultimate nature, our discussion is in terms of consciousness. Spiritual evolution is a conscious process, not an unconscious one. It is because this aspect of man is discussed in ethics that we have a tendency to forget that consciousness is not something unique to the human species, though self-consciousness probably is. Notwithstanding the emphasis that the Jaina tradition lays on the self-conscious aspect of man it consistently maintains that consciousness as such does not have a break, be it the transition from the plant level to the animal level or from the animal to the human and super-human levels. It is in this sense that Jainism talks of two main categories of existence—*jīva* and *ajīva*—the conscious and the non-conscious. Since however the universe of discourse in ethics is the human potentialities and propensities, it looks as if we cannot conceive of man being lowered, however bad he may be. But, the Jaina philosophers' referring to the conscious principle has the wholesome effect of making us ponder over the conscious principle in the universe and of making us trace the evolution

[8] VIII. 9. 41

of consciousness not from the human level alone but from the very stage of 'its coming into existence'. In this emphasis on taking an integral view of consciousness we see that far from laying less emphasis on human responsibility there is a consistent exhortation for man to live really a life worthy of his stage of evolution, first to see that he maintains the level without slipping down and then to aim at the higher evolution of his consciousness.

In the *Uttarādhyayana-Sūtra* we have an interesting illustration of this essential principle of integral consciousness that we find in Jainism. The illustration is this : Three merchants, each having his own capital started business in a place other than their own. One of them recorded considerable gain, the second man returned home with the capital without either gain or loss and the third returned home after losing his capital.[9] In the illustration the capital stands for human life, the gain stands for attainment of heavenly bliss and the loss stands for retrogression into the animal state or suffering the hellish unhappiness. The person who comes back home without loss or gain stands for one who is born a human being in his next birth also. "Those who through the exercise of various virtues become pious house-holders, will be born again as men, for all beings will reap the fruits of their actions. But he who increases his capital is like one who practises eminent virtues. The virtuous, excellent man cheerfully attains the state of gods ... He who practises evil acts and does not fulfill his duty will be born in hell ...A wise man is he who weighs in his mind the state of the sinner and that of the virtuous. Quitting the state of the sinner, the wise realizes that of the virtuous"[10].

It is evident then that the Jaina philosophers' view of metempsychosis not merely emphasizes the eternality of the human soul and hence also the possibility of progress and retrogression but also points to the continuity of consciousness and above all the *responsible nature of the human situation*. In this sense the theory of metempsychosis provides the foundation for Jaina ethics. This will become evident when we consider certain aspects of Jaina ethics in a later chapter.

[9] VII. 14-15
[10] *Ibid.*, VII. 20-21 ; 28; 30

PART IV

METAPHYSICS

19

Reality and Existence

'REALITY' as the key-concept in Metaphysics is an extremely comprehensive term and includes in it a general philosophy of life and a definite view of the universe. It is because of this that the metaphysical aspect of any philosophical system under study is considered as reflecting a 'world-view' of which the outlook on life around forms an integral part.

According to Jainism a proper understanding of Reality consists in comprehending consciousness and matter, for, they both exist. Leaving out of account either of this is, to say the least, taking a partial view of Reality, and, as such, to have an incomplete picture.

The 'hard-core realism' of Jainism is evident from its identification of Reality with Existence. It maintains that Reality is Existence and Existence is Real. The emphasis on taking into consideration both the conscious and the non-conscious aspects (*jīva* and *ajīva*) of Reality on the ground that they both exist points to the fact that the individual soul, matter, space, time and the principles of motion and rest found in the universe are all *Real*.[1] These constitute the *existent reality* and are respectively referred to as *Jīva, Pudgala, Ākāśa, Kāla, Ḍharma* and *Adharma*.[2] The last five together are referred to as *Ajīva*.

[1] See *Bhagavatī-Sūtra*, XXV. 2-4

[2] It should also be noted that in an earlier chapter of the *Bhagavatī-Sūtra* (XIII, 4 & 481) we find the view that the Universe is constituted of five substances. The view is attributed to Mahāvīra himself, who, in reply to one of his

If we refer to *Jīva* and *Ajīva* as the two principles constituting Reality, Jainism may be referred to as a dualistic system. The system may be described also as pluralistic inasmuch as the principle of *Ajīva* itself is understood with the help of the five categories that come under it.

In Jainism the categories which are existent, real and are related to space by being in it are referred to as *astikāyas*. There are in all five *astikāyas*, viz., *jīva*, *pudgala*, *dharma*, *adharma* and *ākāśa*. Another aspect of the *astikāyas* is that they are all manifested in their changing modes and differing qualities. The most important significance of *astikāya* is that it has existence and is also extensive.[3]

Kāla is not considered as an *astikāya* since it certainly is not 'in' space, though coeval with it. But for this it shares the other properties possessed by the other categories. The five *astikāyas* along with *kāla* are the six ultimate categories accepted in Jainism. The term Substance or *Dravya* is made use of to denote the six categories. Since all the six categories are existent, are capable of assuming different modes and exhibit varying qualities, the definition of *dravya* that we find in Jainism is this : "That which maintains its identity while manifesting its various qualities and modifications and which is not different from *sattā* is called *dravya*."[4]

The three aspects of substance mentioned above are extremely significant since they all point to the realism of the Jaina philosophy. The term existence (*sat*) signifies the substantiality of the world outside the perceiver's mind. The world of matter and non-matter is not a mere construction of the mind. It has its independent existence in *rerum natura*. The *Sarvārthasiddhi* points out that essentially substance does not change.[5] The terms 'origin' and 'decay' only refer to the *changing modes* of the substance which in

disciples, Gautama, is believed to have said : "Gautama, the Universe is composed of the five extensive substances. They are the medium of motion, the medium of rest, space, soul and matter." From the fact that a separate place was given to *time* in the same work, it can be inferred that even at the time of Mahāvīra there were two schools of thought in Jainism. This two-fold reference to Reality is significant also in this respect that the first five were considered to be extensive and the sixth, as non-extensive.

[3] *Dravya-saṅgraha*, 24

[4] *Pañcāstikāya*, 8

[5] V. 30

itself is neither created nor destroyed. The eternality of substance is emphasized. The essential nature of clay remaining unchanged among its various modes is cited.

Thus, the 'core' of Existence, the 'entity that endures' is the Substance, and the term *dhruva* is made use of by the Jainas to refer to the aspect of identity. The main argument of the Jainas is that attempting to understand the changes that take place in a thing presupposes that the thing itself persists in spite of the changes. The changing modes of the thing are referred to as *utpāda* and *vyaya*, the terms respectively denoting 'appearance' and 'disappearance'. Umāswāmi defines *sat* as possessing origination, decay and permanence.[6] The terms: modification, becoming, difference, discreetness, plurality, manyness, manifoldness, the occurrent are some of the epithets used in different contexts as synonymns of change (*pāryāya*) which point not merely to productivity (*utpāda*) but to destructibility (*vyaya*) as well. Similarly the terms substantiality, substratum, being, identity, non-difference, continuance, unity, oneness, the continuant, statism, endurance and persistence are used as equivalents to the term permanence (*dhruvatva*).[7]

In terms of the varied reference to Reality in the Jaina tradition, it is obvious, appearance (*utpāda*) and disappearance (*vyaya*) point to the dynamic aspect of Reality and endurance (*dhruva*) refers to the static aspect. It is also logical to maintain that to think of Reality bereft of even any one of the three aspects referred to above is symptomatic of a theoretical abstraction that philosophers have sometimes a tendency to indulge in. Nothing that is real can be thought of without the triple constituents of *utpāda*, *vyaya* and *dhruva*.

The Jaina philosophy of being may be analysed in a slightly different way also. The very assertion of the existence of varying qualities implies something that exists, something of which the existence of varying qualities is postulated. The Jaina point of view is that to speak meaningfully of qualities is synonymous with asserting the existence of a substratum, an entity which is at the base. The assertion of a substance is also implied in considering the changing modes, for the changes and the modes must be of some-

[6] *Tattvārtha-Sūtra*, V. 29

[7] See Y.J. Padmarajiah, *Jaina Theories of Reality and Knowledge* (Bombay: Jain Sahitya Vikas Mandal, 1963), p. 127

thing and that something persists and hence is as real as the changing modes and qualities.

Jaina ontology rests on the theory of identity and change outlined above. The Jaina view comes into bold relief when we contrast it with other points of view expressed in the Indian tradition itself, views which have naturally been critical of Jainism. In the absence of a proper understanding of the distinguishing feature of Jainism it is natural to expect the charge of self-contradiction against the identity-and-difference view of Reality and Existence. We shall dwell at some length on the various views on Reality in the next chapter. Here we shall make a pointed reference to the fact that even a serious student of Jainism like Jacobi has pointed to a lack of a central idea upholding a mass of philosophical tenets. While commencing his address to the Third International Congress for the History of Religions in 1908 he said : "All those who approach Jaina philosophy will be under the impression that it is a mass of philosophical tenets not upheld by one central idea, and they will wonder what could have given currency to what appears to us an unsystematical system."[8] From our point of view the words that follow are extremely significant, for Jacobi continued : "I myself have held, and given expression to this opinion[9] but I have now learned to look at Jaina philosophy in a different light. It has, I think, a metaphysical basis of its own, which secured it a position apart from the rival systems both of the Brahmans and of the Buddhists."[10] The fact that even a scholar like Jacobi was initially critical of Jaina metaphysics and later appreciated the integrated pattern of Jaina thought as a whole re-assures us that an open-minded approach to the Jaina system is bound to result in a proper understanding of Jaina metaphysics.

One other aspect of Jaina metaphysics needs to be touched here before we pass on to contrast it with other systems of Indian thought. From the discussion of the Jaina concept of Reality, Exis-

[8] Jaina Vijaya Muni, edt., *Studies in Jainism* (Ahmedabad : Jaina Sahitya Samsodhaka Studies, 1946), p. 48

[9] In his Introduction to his edition of the *Kalpa-Sūtra* (p. 3) he wrote that Mahāvīra's philosophy "scarcely forms a system, but is merely a sum of opinions (*pannatis*) on various subjects, no fundamental ideas being there to uphold the mass of philosophical matter."

[10] Jina Vijaya Muni, edt., *op. cit.*, p. 48

tence and Substance, it is evident that just as Reality and Existence are identified, Reality and Substance are also identified in Jainism. This is expressed in a cryptic proposition that is found in a Jaina classic : "All is one because all exists."[11]

It should, however be understood that this identity is valid only from the transcendental point of view (*dravyārthika-naya*) and not from the empirical standpoint (*paryāyārthika-naya*). From the latter point of view the division of substance into the *jīva* and the *ajīva* and of the sub-division of *ajīva* into the other five categories is alone valid.

[11] *Taṭtvārtha-Sūtra bhāṣyā*, I. 35

20

Ontology

THE Jaina system adopts neither of the extreme positions in regard to the theory of being—either emphasizing *Identity* or describing *Difference* as pointing to the essential nature of Reality. Nor does it take the position of considering either identity or difference as more important in understanding Reality. In Jainism we find an acceptance of both identity and difference as equally significant in comprehending Reality. There is a stubborn refusal to take up any one of the extreme positions or even the position belittling the importance of either identity or difference. The Jaina view of Reality can best be understood against the backdrop that a brief survey of the ontological positions taken by some of the schools of Indian thought provides. At the one extreme end is the Advaita school of Śaṅkara which maintains Identity as Reality and at the other extreme is the Buddhist view which considers Difference as constituting the essence of Reality. Between these two are the views of Sāṅkhya and the Viśiṣṭādvaita systems in which difference is subordinated to identity and the position of the Vaiśeṣika and Dvaita systems which subordinates identity to difference. We shall review the schools in order.

The Advaita view is that *Brahman* is the one ultimate Reality and the empirical world is only a phenomenon. The plurality or difference experienced by us does not give us an idea of Reality, it only points to *Brahman* which is at its base. The phenomenal world does not represent a real transformation (*pariṇāma*) of its material cause ; it is only an appearance. The non-dual *Brahman* which is the one Reality appears as the world.

Śaṅkara's whole conception of the Universe is built upon his doctrine of *vivarta* or appearance of the Real into something which is not. The rope-snake analogy is very effectively used by Śaṅkara to illustrate his view-point that what *seems* to be real need not necessarily be real. In the example, the rope is real, and the snake is not. All the same the rope-snake seems to possess all the characteristics of the real snake. The reason for this fact is not understood, the rope which is really there is not comprehended, but only the snake which is not there. On the dawn of real knowledge (in this case the knowledge that there is only a rope and not a snake) the rope is not seen as a snake at all. From the point of view of the person who has a true knowledge of the situation, there is no snake, there is only the rope. Similarly, the only Reality, *Brahman* appears as the world and as long as this fact is not understood the plurality of the universe is asserted and considered to represent the whole of Reality. Śaṅkara's insistence is on passing from the plurality of the universe which is only apparent and not real to the non-duality of *Brahman* which is the only Real in the universe, which appeared as the world of animate beings and inanimate objects. Śaṅkara thus maintains that *Brahman* is the sole reality which admits of no difference. His ontological view is one of pure, homogeneous being.

The Buddhist view of Reality is diametrically opposed to that of the Advaita. Notions like permanence (*nityatva*), identity (*tadātmya*), generality (*sāmānya*) are products of imagination (*kalpanā*) according to the Buddhists. As against the term soul (*ātman*), eternality (*nityatva*) and bliss (*ānanda*) found in the Upaniṣads to describe Reality, we find the terms soulless (*nairātmya*), impermanence (*anitya*) and suffering (*dukkha*) in the Buddhist canons to point to Reality and the view of life it implies. The notion of difference, the corollary of the view of impermanence, the characteristic feature of the Buddhist ontology is clearly stated by Th. Stcherbastsky when he says : "The sole and ultimately real in Buddhism, is the 'point-instant' or 'the moment' (*kṣaṇa*). Each moment is different from or 'other' than the rest in the series (*santāna*). Whatsoever (exists) exists separately (*sarvaṁ prthate*) from 'other' existing things. To exist means to exist separately. . . The notion of 'apartness' belongs to the essential feature of the notion of existence (*bhāvalakṣaṇapṛthaktvāt*)."[1] "Thus every reality is another reality. What is identical or similar is not ultimately real."[2] Stcherbastsky adds in this connection that "a difference in space-time is a difference in substance."[3]

The notion of an enduring substance is denied by the Buddhists. The 'moments' alone are real and the continuity-ideas associated with them as forming their connecting links are all our mind's creation. Difference is thus the key-note in the Buddhist metaphysics. If the notion of continuity which gives rise to the notion of permanence, substantiality and identity is not accepted, the reason is that each existence is entirely autonomous and independent.

In the Sāṅkhya system is discernible a serious attempt at getting over the problems concerning bare identity or being and total change or an eternal becoming by synthesizing them. The clue to the Sāṅkhya view is to be found in the dualism posited between matter and consciousness, referred to as *prakṛti* and *puruṣa*. These represent the two important but independent aspects of Reality, *prakṛti* standing for the dynamic but non-conscious principle and *puruṣa* representing the static but conscious. Since *prakṛti* is the dynamic entity it is responsible for all changes that take place in nature. The changes are attributable to the different types of combinations of *sattva*, *rajas* and *tamas*, the ultimate constituents of *prakṛti*. Both the evolution of different things and the dissolution point to the reality of change. In the former case more and more differentiation takes place giving rise to diverse kinds of evolutes. In the latter case, the various things constituting the universe disintegrate and the original state of undifferentiated homogeneity is facilitated to be regained. Change is thus real in this system.

The concept of change which points to the notion of difference, however can be understood only in the light of the *satkāryavāda* theory of causality held by the Sāṅkhyas. According to this view the effect is not something entirely different from the cause ; it is something present in the cause right from the beginning. The usual example given is that of the yarns and the fabric, the fabric as the effect being considered as having been already present in the yarns,

1 *Buddhist Logic* (Leningrad, 1930), Vol. I, p. 30

2 *Ibid.*, Vol. I, p. 105

3 *Ibid.*, Vol. II, p. 282f.

the cause. The difference between the cause and the effect is that the latter connotes a specific type of arrangement (*saṁsthānabheda*) of the former. The element of identity found between the cause and the effect is considered to have such a lot of significance in the system that the importance of difference itself gets diminished.

Viśiṣṭādvaita : The very name of the system, viz., qualified non-dualism indicates to us the view of Reality that it takes. Reality or *Brahman* is not non-dual but is a complex whole which incorporates within itself unity as well as diversity. In contrast to Śaṅkara's view of absolute identity in which difference gets obliterated, in Rāmānuja's system difference is not set aside as a mere construction of the mind, and therefore as illusory, but as being integrated with an abiding entity.

The complex whole is constituted of the ultimate triad, *acit*, *cit* and *Īśvara* respectively standing for the principle of material objects, the principle of individual spirits and God. The relationship between God on the one hand and *cit* and *acit* on the other is analogous to that which holds between a substance and its attributes. The attributes themselves do not have significance apart from the substance but all the same they are different from God just as a body is different from it soul. The Absolute is thus a complex which consists of one cosmic soul and its dependents — the world and the individual selves — which serve its purpose. P. N. Srinivasachari notes the significant distinction between the Viśiṣṭādvaita view of difference and the Buddhistic and Advaita views on the other : "The Buddhist view of quality without substance is countered by the monistic view of substance without qualities and these extremes find their reconciliation in the Viśiṣṭādvaita theory of the world as the *viśeṣaṇa* of *Brahman*."[4]

Vaiśeṣika view : The system is known for its emphasis on difference or *viśeṣa*, and the significant fact is that difference is referred to as one of the six categories of Reality. The categories are : substance (*dravya*), quality (*guṇa*), activity (*karma*), generality (*sāmānya*), difference (*viśeṣa*) and intimate relation (*samavāya*). From the fact that the system itself is designated after the ontological principle of difference, it is obvious that *viśeṣa* is not treated as one among the other categories, however significant the inclusion

[4] *Viśiṣṭādvaita*, p. 230f.

of it in the list of categories itself may be. Garbe observes: "Difference (*viśeṣa*), the fifth category . . . holds an important place in the Vaiśeṣika system inasmuch as, by virtue of it the difference of the atoms renders possible the formation of the universe. The name, therefore, of the entire system, Vaiśeṣika, is derived from the word for difference (*viśeṣa*)."[5]

The Vaiśeṣika's fundamental position is that no entity constituting Reality can be conceived of without understanding the *viśesa* rooted in it. Differentiating *one* entity from *all the* others itself is possible because of its *viśesa* or particularity. The introduction of the concept of intimate relation (*samavāya*) by the Vaiśeṣika philosopher distinguishes the system itself from the Buddhist philosophy which holds on to the view-point of 'total difference'. This is evident from the unique and discrete particular doctrine (*svalakṣaṇa-vāda*). *Samavāya* is a synthesizing principle and does not enjoy the status of introducing changes between the relata. As such, the emphasis on difference is maintained and identity is kept at bay.

Dvaita view: The emphasis on the principle of difference in the Dvaita system is apparent from the division of categories into the Independent (*svatantra*) and the Dependent (*paratantra*). God is the only independent substance and the individual souls and the material world are dependent on Him. The whole tenor of the Dvaita view is that the individual soul (and the world) are different from the Supreme Lord and, understanding the situation of fundamental difference between the individual soul and God is the essential preliminary for realizing *mokṣa*. The *ātman* is said to be 'not that', and the *māhāvākya* signifies essentially the distinction that exists between the individual soul and the universal soul. The importance attached to difference in the Dvaita system is pointed out by one of the exponents of the system who writes: "An individual or an object is what it is in virtue of its difference from other objects belonging to the same class or genus and difference *ipso facto* from members of another class or genus. Whether the linguistic medium is used or not, whether there is outward expression or not, difference is the essential constituent of an object or individual. An object is what it is only on account of its difference from other objects. In accordance with the pragmatic purpose of the subject,

[5] Article on Vaiśeṣika, *Encyclopaedia of Religion and Ethics*, Vol 12, p. 570

and in accordance with the fundamental and essential constitution of the objects themselves, difference is stressed. It is difference that lends significance to identity."[6]

It is evident from the above that even to identify an object understanding its distinctive features is essential. In a sense no doubt the substance and its attributes are identical, but they are not completely so ; it is because of this that we are able to meaningfully refer to the distinction between a substance and its attributes. The import of all this is that difference rather than identity is considered important in the metaphysical system of Dvaita.

A review of the different types of metaphysical theories has impressed on us the fact that Reality is sought to be identified or equated with either pure unity or uncompromising diversity. In case the extreme views are not adopted the reason for the same is to be found in the system considering either of the concepts (unity or diversity) as more significant in describing Reality.

Jainism is against taking up such definite positions, and the reason is as simple as it is revealing. It is simple since there is no mincing of matters and no abstraction is indulged in. It is revealing because the common man and the philosopher will find in it an echo of their voice. Reality is so complex that it is difficult to precisely indicate its nature, maintains the Jaina philosopher. If so, to emphatically maintain that Reality must be construed in a specific way, precluding all the other approaches to it is making simple that which is complex. The complex nature of the Real cannot be revealed fully by simple propositions — propositions formulated by different schools and claimed as the only valid ones. The man in the street and the philosopher concede that Reality is complex. Whereas the former is so desperate that he gives up the task of philosophizing about Reality, the latter is so bold as to suggest definitive solutions to unravel the metaphysical problem. The Jaina philosopher proves to be the exception inasmuch as he suggests that identity, permanence and change are all true and real.

It is suggested by a scholar that "productivity and destructibility constitute the two aspects of change and may, therefore, be together characterized as the dynamic aspect of reality, the static aspect

[6] R. Nagaraja Sarma, *Reign of Religion in Indian Philosophy*, p. 239

being represented by permanence."[7] He refers to Indrabhūti's questions and Mahāvīra's answers in support of his statement. On being asked by Indrabhūti, his foremost apostle (*gaṇadhara*) : "What is the nature of reality?" (*kiṁ tattvam*), Mahāvīra is reported to have first answered 'origination' and then after the same question was successively repeated, 'destruction' and 'persistence.'[8]

A careful observation of Reality reveals that not only substance but its changing modes as well are real, asserts the Jaina philosopher. The consistent realism of the Jaina tradition is reflected in its discussion of the various categories it accepts as constituting Reality. We shall now consider the categories in some detail.

[7] Y.J. Padmarajiah, *op. cit.*, p. 127

[8] *Ibid.*, p. 127 f.n.

21

Jiva

THE Jainas consider that there are six real categories constituting Substance, viz., Soul (*Jīva*), Matter (*Pudgala*), Principle of Motion (*Dharma*), Principle of Rest (*Adharma*), Space (*Ākāśa*) and Time (*Kāla*). Since all the categories are real and independent, they are also referred to as the substances (*dravyas*).

Of these, *jīva* is conscious but has no form,[1] *pudgala* is non-conscious but has form and *dharma*, *adharma*, *ākāśa* and *kāla* are non-conscious and formless.[2] Jainism thus holds the view that Reality is divisible not merely into two general categories—the conscious and the material—but into three,—the conscious, the material and a category which is both unconscious and immaterial. In the *Bhagavatī-Sūtra* we find the two-fold classification of substance into the *rūpin* (with form) and the *arūpin* (formless) . . . but there is absolutely no difference in regard to the enumeration of the categories themselves. This is evident from the fact that under *rūpin* is included *pudgala* and under *arūpin* are included the other categories. We shall briefly consider the specific qualities and modes of the six *dravyas*. It is convenient to consider first the category of *jīva* and then *ajīva* under which are included the other five categories.

JĪVA : The Jaina system maintains that the *jīva* is real and eternal (uncreated and indestructible) and that there are an infinite number of them, all imperceptible because of their formlessness.

[1] *Tattvārtha-Sūtra,* V. 5

[2] *Ibid.,* V. 4

The most distinguishing characteristic of this category is the possession of consciousness (*cetanā*) and this enables the *jīva* to get both the indeterminate and the determinate types of knowledge (*darśana* and *jñāna*).

The term *jīva* does not refer to the human soul alone. It refers to the principle of consciousness in general. Consciousness is discernible in four different states of existence (*gati*) according to Jainism. The different levels of consciousness representing the various states of existence are that of the animals,[3] the humans, the infernal beings and the celestial beings. The *svastikā* sign which we constantly see in the Jaina books and in the Jaina temples signifies the four different states of existence of the *jīva* :

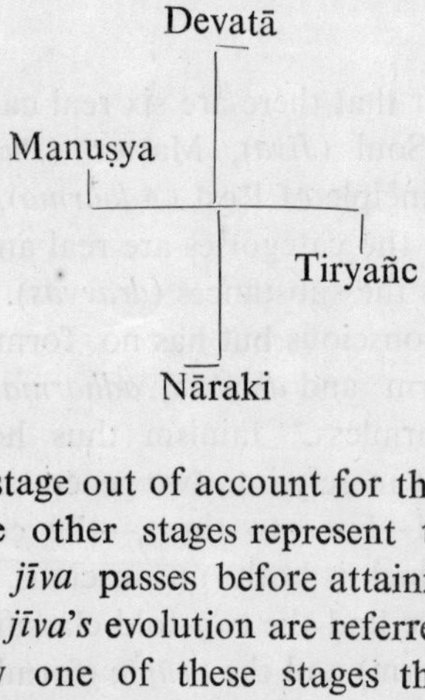

Leaving the *Nāraki* stage out of account for the moment it may be pointed out that the other stages represent the progressive steps through which the *jīva* passes before attaining perfection. These various stages of the *jīva's* evolution are referred to as the 'modes' or *paryāyas*. In every one of these stages the *jīva* undergoes real changes, though its identity itself is not lost. The changes are seen in the facts of birth, growth and death.

Due to its association with *karma* the *jīva* gets bound and is caught up in the cycle of birth and death. Association with *karma* is considered to be a mark of impurity and hence the *jīva* in the state of bondage is referred to as impure (*aśuddha*). With the attainment

[3] That the term 'animal' did not exclude the plant-level is evident from the definition of animal as "those beings which remain in the celestial, the infernal and the 'human world' ". That we find in the *Tattvārtha-Sūtra* (IV. 28). This definition of animal and of the concept of consciousness offers us an insight into the seemingly rigorous doctrine of *ahiṁsā* which excludes injury even to plants and seeds that we find in Jainism.

of liberation (*mokṣa*) the *jīva* becomes pure (*śuddha*). Though we have referred to two types of *jīva*, *aśuddhā jīva* and *śuddha jīva* it is well to remember that the two are not entirely different from each other. This can be substantiated by comparing the qualities possessed by the two types of *jīvas* :

	AŚUDHA JĪVA	*ŚUDHA JĪVA*
1.	Possesses consciousness (*cetanā*) but only to a limited extent.	This is nothing but perfect, unlimited consciousness.
2.	Possesses the capacity for apprehension and comprehension.	Apprehension and comprehension are developed to the fullest extent and they are considered to become identical with each other.
3.	Has lordship (*prabhutva*), i. e., it has the capacity to take different states of existence through life.	Enjoys perfect sovereignty.
4.	Has the capacity to act. Has freedom of the will. Hence it is known as the doer (*kartā*).	Has a complete mastery over *karma*. So it is *kartā* in the truest sense of the term.
5.	It is an enjoyer (*bhokta*).	It is the enjoyer in the full sense of the term. It enjoys transcendent bliss.
6.	Possesses just the size of the body it happens to occupy (*dehamātra*).	Spiritual nature is fully realized.
7.	Has no corporeal form (*amūrta*), yet associated with a kārmic body.	Completely devoid of corporeal form, the *jīva* having destroyed the kārmic body.
8.	It is always in association with *karma*. (*karma saṁyukta*).	It is completely free from *karma*, the *jīva* having destroyed the kārmic body.
9.	Has life with all the life-principles.	Is the pure and perfected self.

From the enumeration of the qualities possessed by the two types of *jīva* it is clear that the *śuddha jīva* is not something distinct from or opposed to *aśuddha jīva*.

The *aśuddha jīvas* are classified into two types — non-moving (*sthāvara*) and moving (*trasa*). The non-moving are considered to be one-sensed (possessing the tactual sensation alone) and are said to be of five types : living respectively in the bodies of earth (*pṛithvikāya*), water (*apkāya*), fire (*tejaskāya*), air (*vāyukāya*) and vegetable (*vanaspatikāya*). The finer types cannot be perceived by the sense organs.

Examples for the first type are dust, clay, sand, stones, metals, vermilion, orpiment; for the second type : water, dew, snow, fog; for the third type : flames, coals, meteors, lightning; for the fourth type : squalls, whirlwinds; for the fifth type : those who have, together with others, a common body — as garlic and onion, those who have their own body as trees, shrubs, etc.[4]

The moving *jīvas* are classified into the two-sensed (possessing the senses of touch and taste), the three-sensed (possessing the senses of touch, taste and sight), the four-sensed (possessing the senses of touch, taste, sight and smell) and the five-sensed (possessing the senses of touch, taste, sight, smell and hearing).

Examples for the two-sensed *jīvas* are : worms, shells, leeches; for the three-sensed : bugs, ants and cochineals[5] and moths; for the four-sensed : bees, flies, mosquitoes. The five-sensed *jīvas* are considered to be of three types : acquatic animals such as fishes and dolphins, terrestrial animals such as elephants, and air animals such as gees. These are all divisible into beings with reason (*saṁjñin*) and those without reason (*asaṁjñin*). The *Tattvārtha-Sūtra* defines the reasoning beings as "those endowed with an inner sense."[6] The five-sensed animals which are womb-born, e.g., cattle, goats, sheep, elephants, lions and tigers are considered to possess reason.[7] The

[4] See Jacobi, edt., *Jaina Sūtras*, II, p. 215 seq.

[5] Illustrating the importance accorded to this class in practical life by the Jainas, Mrs. Sinclair Stevenson in *The Heart of Jainism*, p. 100 writes : "A Jaina told me that in order to please the insects of this class a devout householder when he finds vermin will often place them on one particular bedstead and then pay some poor person from four to six annas to spend the night on that bedstead. Others, however, deny this. Of course, no true Jaina will kill vermin, but will carefully remove it from his body or house to some shady place outside where it can dwell in safety. They say that, far from killing vermin, they are bound to protect it, as it has been created through their lack of cleanliness."

[6] *Tattvārtha-Sūtra,* II. 25

[7] *Ibid*

asaṁjñins are instinctive.

The Human State of Existence : The general division of mankind is into those who are in some sense infirm, i. e , those in whom not all organs and faculties have fully grown and those in whom all the physical organs and psychical faculties are well-developed. The latter have the greatest advantage in the matter of attaining liberation, for, self-discipline, the pre-requisite for salvation is possible only for beings whose sensory and mental organs are fully developed. In this sense we see the recognition given to the state of well-being—both physical and mental—so essential for even turning the human species towards the aspiration for release from the cycle of birth and death. When there is physical ill-health or infirmity or mental ill-health, the mental equipoise,—the *sine qua non* for ethical preparation—is just not possible.

The Celestial State : Gods (*devas*), when compared to human beings have long lives enjoying different states of bliss. The state of godhood is not the 'end-state' according to Jainism. Even the gods do not enjoy an infinite state of bliss or birthlessness. They are also reborn as human beings or as animals, according to their *karma.* According to the *karmas* they 'appear' through 'manifestation' (*utpāda*) and such a state of existence also comes to an end when the *karmas* are ended. Here again they differ from the human beings in that, unlike the latter, there is no determining cause of death, terminating their state of existence in a particular mode. The characteristic feature of godly existence is stated to consist in their faculties—both physical and mental—being fully developed.[8]

The celestial beings are classified into four types ;

(1) The *Bhāvanavāsins* : These are considered to belong to the lowest species, and are sub-divided into ten classes.[9]

(2) The *Vyantaras* : These are supposed to live in all three worlds and they are not completely free as is evident from the fact that sometimes they serve even human beings. They are sub-divided into eight groups.[10]

[8] *Karmagrantha*, I. 115b

[9] The ten groups are : *Asura-kumāra, Nāga-Kumāra, Vidyut-Kumāra, Suparṇa-kumāra, Agni-kumāra, Vāta-kumāra, Stanita-kumāra, Udādhi-kumāra, Dvīpa-kumāra,* and *Dik-kumāra.*

[10] The eight classes are : *Kinnara, Kiṁpuruṣa, Mahoraga, Gandharva, Yakṣa,*

(3) The *Jyotiṣkas* : These are divisible into five groups and represent the suns, moons, planets, nakṣatras and fixed stars. Only for the human world they appear to be in a continuous state of motion. The peculiarity of the Jaina doctrine regarding the plurality of suns and moons needs some explanation here. Especially in regard to *Jambūdvīpa* it is considered to have two suns and two moons. "They proceed from the idea that in the course of twenty four hours the sun as well as other heavenly bodies can only make half of the circuit of the Meru, that therefore, when the night in *Bhārata-varṣa* (India) reaches its end, the sun, whose light had given the preceding day, has only reached the north-west of Meru. The sun which rises actually in the east of *Bhārata-varṣa* cannot, therefore, be the same sun which set the previous evening, but is a second, different sun, which however cannot be distinguished by the eye from the first. On the morning of the third day there reappears the first sun which has reached, at about this time, the south-east corner of the Meru. For the same reason the Jainas presume the existence of two moons, two series of *nakṣatras*, etc. All heavenly bodies are thus doubled ; but as only one member of this pair appears always in *Bhārata-varṣa* and as both members completely resemble one another, nothing in the phenomenon is thereby changed."[11]

(4) The *Vaimānikas* which have a two-fold division *kalpopapannas & kalpātitas*. *Kalpa* means 'abode of gods'.[12]

(5) The Infernal State of Existence (*Nāraka*) : This is the state of existence of the *jīva* which is born in hell. It is constantly tormented by heat, cold, hunger, thirst and pain. Hatred is their innate quality and it impels them to entertain bad thoughts and inflict pain on others.

The 'hell beings' inhabit seven successively descending regions underneath the earth.[13] The deeper the layers the *jīva* inhabits, the more horrible is its appearance and the more unbearable are the

Rākṣasa, *Bhūta* and *Piśāca*.

[11] G. Thibaut, *Astronomie* (in Grunoriss der indo-arischen Philologie, Vol. III Nv. 9), p. 21 seq.

Cited in Helmuth von Glasenapp, *The Doctrine of Karman in Jaina Philosophy*, p. 59

[12] *Tattvārtha-Sūtra*, IV. 1-27

[13] The 'seven hells' are : Ratnaprabhā, Sarkāraprabhā, Valukaprabhā, Pankaprabhā, Dhūmaprabhā, Tamahprabhā, and Mahātamahprabhā.

sufferings it has to undergo. The first three hells are considered to be hot, the next, both hot and cold and the last two, cold.

The four states of the *jīva* described above has impressed on us the Jaina view that there is continuity of consciousness from the lowest of animate beings to the highest stage of perfection in which purity of consciousness is regained,—the stage which is clearly far above the ordinary human level. The logic of such a theory of consciousness is that at no stage is any *jiva* to be despised or looked down upon. More often than not, this fundamental truth about the state of human existence—that it is only an intermediate stage towards perfection is forgotten. The result is that man is given so much of importance that the sub-human species is ignored completely. The Jaina theory of consciousness, in keeping with its logic of continuity of consciousness insists on *reverence for life*, to use the terminology of Albert Schweitzer. The result is that a strong foundation is laid for a severe and a necessary ethic of *ahiṁsā*, the high-watermark of Jaina philosophy and culture. This will be discussed in a later chapter.

22

Ajiva

THE term *Ajīva* is used to denote the five categories of *pudgala*, *dharma*, *adharma*, *ākāśa* and *kāla*. We shall consider them in order.

PUDGALA : This category denotes matter or material objects in general. Matter is uncreated, indestructible and real ; so, the material world is not a 'figment of imagination' but is substantially real, real independently of the perceiving mind. The deep significance of Jaina realism becomes easily understood when we reflect about the general philosophy of realism.

The touch-stone for assessing the realistic aspect of any philosophical system is its conception of matter. The recognized and universally accepted method of interrogation in this context is whether the world really exists or not. From the point of view of the individual who analyses the issue, the specific question is : "Does the world outside him, i.e., outside his perceiving mind exist or not ?" If the answer is that it exists, — exists independently of his own perception — it is symptomatic of the realist view ; if not, it indicates an idealistic conception. The basic definition of *pudgala* which stands for matter in Jainism is "that which can be experienced by the five sense organs." Knowledge derived by the sense organs is of the outside world, and since each sense organ is capable of giving the perceiver one type of knowledge of the outside world, the sum-total of the knowledge derived represents the various aspects of the world outside. The visual organ, for instance conveys information about the colour and shape of the objects constituting the external world; similarly the tactual sense organ 'communicates' to the individual whether the object 'it is in touch with' is hard or soft. The other sense organs similarly make awareness of the other aspects of the world possible. It is in the light of this that the term 'experienced by the sense organs' should be understood. Since experience establishes contact with the outside world and matter as the object of experience reveals the nature to the perceiver, the significance of the Jaina definition of matter is that it makes the realistic position of the system unambiguously clear.

A second definition of matter we find in Jainism not only confirms the realistic position but, consistently with it, reveals also the dynamic conception of Reality. The definition is arrived at from the etymology of the compound word *pudgala.* The term *pud* refers to the process of combination and *gala* stands for dissociation. Matter is said to be that which undergoes modifications by combinations and dissociations. The exact significance of this definition can be gathered by analysing the Jaina view of the ultimate constituents of matter.

In determining the ultimate constituents of matter the method of division is helpful. When any object is divided, the parts obtained by division can be further divided but the process of division itself cannot be indefinitely continued ; for, in the process a position is reached when no further division is possible. This is truly the ultimate constituent of matter, — referred to by the term *aṇu* or *paramāṇu* (atom) — in Jaina philosophy.[1] The implication of such a reference is that the atom itself is not produced by the combination of smaller constituents. The position is made more explicit in another source-book which states that "the atoms are produced only by division of matter ; not by the process of union or combination."[2] The process of combination of the atoms gives rise to the molecules referred to as *skandha* in Jainism. It is the combination of molecules that is responsible for the different types of objects, possessing varying qualities. The main difference between the atoms and the molecules consists in the fact that the former are not further divisible and are only capable of combining to produce the latter ; the former is imperceptible and the latter is perceptible. The molecules, however are not merely capable of division, reducing

1 *Sarvārthasiddhi,* V. 25
2 *Tattvārtha-Sūtra,* V. 27

themselves into atoms ; they are also capable of combining with each other to produce the various objects. It should however be noted here that it is also held that "out of molecules composed of even a large number of atoms, some are visible and some invisible."[3] It is held that the visibility or general perceivability of the molecules is dependent on the combined process of division and addition. It is maintained : "If a molecule breaks and the broken part then attaches itself to another molecule, the resulting combination may be coarse enough to be perceived."[4] A Jaina scholar cites, in support of the view, the example of the molecules of hydrogen and chlorine which are themselves invisible to the eyes but which by breaking and combining to form two molecules of hydrochloric acid become visible."[5]

Six forms of *skandha* are recognized :[6]

(i) *Bhadra-bhadra* : This type of *skandha*, when split cannot regain the original, undivided form. Solids are typical examples.

(ii) *Bhadra* : When split this type of *skandha* has the capacity to join together. Liquids are the examples cited.

(ii) *Bhadra-Sūkṣma* : This type of *skandha* appears gross but is really subtle, as is evident from the fact that it can neither be split nor is capable of being pierced through or taken up in hand. Examples cited are : sun, heat, shadow, light, darkness, etc. Minute particles of these are evident to the senses.

(iv) *Sūkṣma-bhadra* : This type of *skandha* also appears gross but is also subtle. Examples cited are : sensations of touch, smell, colour and sound.

(v) & (vi) Both are extremely subtle and beyond sense-perception. The particles of *karma* are cited as examples.

The molecules possess five characteristics, viz., touch, taste, smell, sound and colour. It is because of the characteristics that we perceive the various qualities. The atoms themselves are not qualitatively different. In this respect the Jaina theory of atoms is different from that of the Vaiśeṣika theory which accepts qualitative differences in the atoms.

3 *Sarvārthasiddhi*, V. 28

4 *Ibid*

5 *Outlines of Jaina Philosophy*, p. 74

6 See A. Chakravarti, *Religion of Ahiṁsā* (Bombay : Ratanchand Hirachand, 1957), p. 117

It is obvious then that the Jaina view of Reality as Identity and Change is clearly reflected in its atomic theory. The changes we experience in the objects are due to the different modes of combination of the atoms and these are referred to as the changing modes of the objects. But underlying all the changing modes is the fact that there is the identity of the ultimate constituents, the atoms. The atoms themselves do not change, only the modes of their combinations undergo that change, producing the various modes of the objects. In terms, therefore, of the atoms, it may be said that in them as ultimate constituents, we find the Identity element in Reality, and in their combining to form molecules and in the latter's division and addition we find the element of Change.

DHARMA : This is the principle of motion and pervades the whole universe. This represents the indispensable and necessary condition of motion of objects in the universe, though it does not make the objects move. It is only the medium of motion ; it itself does not move. Mehta writes: "The medium of motion does not create motion but only helps them who have already got the capacity of moving . . . As water helps fish in swimming, the *jivāstikāya – pudgalāstikāya* are helped by *dharmāstikāya* when the former tend to move. The medium of motion is an immaterial substance possessing no consciousness.[7]

Dharma has none of the five sense qualities possessed by *pudgala.* Existence is its nature and hence it is not considered to be a product. From the empirical standpoint it is considered to possess an infinite number of space-points (*pradeśas*), though from the transcendental point of view it is said to possess only one *pradeśa.*

ADHARMA : This is the principle of rest and pervades the whole universe. This is the auxiliary cause of rest to the soul and matter.[8] It is because of this principle that bodies in motion are enabled to enjoy a state of rest. It does not actively interfere with the moving object. In this respect it is like the earth which is the condition of rest for objects on it. It does not positively interfere and arrest the motion of bodies which require rest.

Like *dharma*, *adharma* is also considered to be devoid of the five sense qualities. *Adharma* is also considered to be possessed of an

[7] *Outlines of Jaina Philosophy*, p. 33

[8] *Niyamasāra*, 30

infinite number of *pradeśas*, but this is true only from the empirical point of view. From the transcendental standpoint, it is considered to possess only one *pradeśa*.

Dharma aud *adharma* are considered to be responsible for the systematic character of the universe. Without these there would be only a chaos in the cosmos. We may mention here in passing that this aspect of the theory of *dharma* and *adharma* is similar to the one we find in Hinduism regarding the principle of *dharma* and *adharma*. These two are responsible, according to the Hindu view, for coherence and system in the universe and absence of coherence and system, respectively. But, whereas in Jainism these two are considered to be metaphysical categories, in Hinduism, primarily they are considered to be ethical principles. Since, however, an idealistic ethics has its metaphysical implications and roots, the concepts of *dharma* and *adharma* are considered also in a metaphysical context in Hinduism also.

ĀKĀŚA : This is space and is considered to be objectively real, and as being possessed of an infinite number of space-points, and the latter are imperceptible. Space is considered to be eternal and uncreated.

Space is divided into two : *lokākāśa* and *alokākāśa*. In the former the *dravyas* exist and it roughly corresponds to the common sense view of the universe. In the latter nothing exists. It is pure or 'outer' space. It is beyond *lokākāśa*.[9]

KĀLA : This is time and since it is not 'in space' it is not an *astikāya*. It is coexistent with space. The real substances which constantly change imply a time-duration in which changes take place. Since change is considered as real and not as illusion, time is necessarily considered to be real.

Time is of two types, absolute or real time (*dravya kāla*) and conventional or relative time (*vyavahāra kāla*). The former is understood from the logical notion of continuous, never-ending stream of time[10] and the latter is the one which is helpful in producing changes in a substance. It it therefore known only through the modifications produced on them. Time is also considered to be beginningless.

[9] *Dravya-saṅgraha*, 19
[10] *Ibid.*, 21

23

Nayavada

THE pluralistic realism of the Jainas presupposes the acceptance of the principle of distinction; the distinction, to start with, is of the mind and the world, but in Jainism the principle has been allowed to reach its logical conclusion, resulting in the theory of manifoldness of reality and knowledge. Reality, according to Jainism, is a complex not merely in the sense of constituting manyness (*aneka*) but also because of its manifoldness (*anekānta*). Jainism does not merely maintain that there are many reals but also accepts that each of the reals, in its turn is so complex that it is difficult to understand it fully. The infinite number of qualities possessed by the complex reals and the equal number of relations into which they enter point to the fact that Reality may be comprehended from different angles. The attempt at comprehending anything from a particular standpoint is known as *naya* — a view arrived at from one angle. Dasgupta's translation of the term *nayavāda* into doctrine of relative pluralism is extremely significant since it points to the perspective from which *nayavāda* itself is to be understood. He writes : "The Jains regarded all things as *anekānta* (*na-ekānta*) or in other words they held that nothing could be affirmed absolutely, as all affirmations were true only under certain conditions."[1]

Since Reality can be looked at from an infinite number of standpoints because of the possession of an infinite number of qualities,

[1] *op. cit.*,Vol. I, p. 175

we have an infinite number of *nayas*. But the Jaina philosophers have specifically analysed seven *nayas*. A *naya* is defined as a particular opinion or a view-point — a view-point which does not rule out other different view-points, and is therefore expressive of a partial truth about an object — as entertained by a knowing agent.[2] This is a very general definition of *naya* and the specific nature of each *naya* is sketched in the seven *nayas* formulated by the Jaina philosophers. The seven *nayas* are the *naigama*, *saṅgraha*, *vyavahāra*, *ṛjusūtra*, *śabda*, *samabhirūḍha* and *evaṁbhūta*. We may consider them in some detail.

Naigama Naya : (Universal-Particular, Teleological Standpoint)

An analysis of any object in the universe reveals that it possesses both general (*sāmānya*) and specific (*viśeṣa*) qualities (*guṇa*). The object may thus be rightly looked upon as a complex of the universal and particular attributes. The *naigama naya* does not overlook either the universal or the particular aspect of things. It signifies that we cannot understand the universal without the particular and *vice versa*. The proposition "I am conscious," for example, signifies not merely the individuality of the 'I' but also the universality of the quality 'I' am said to possess, viz., consciousness.

The analysis of non-distinction between the universal and the particular involved in the *naigama naya* is extremely significant. The fact that the universal and the particular are specified as being synthesized means clearly that the Jaina philosophers did not commit the mistake of asserting absolute non-distinction or identity between the two. Distinction is implied clearly, though care is taken to see that it is maintained relatively only. It is from this standpoint that the Jainas were critical of the Nyāya-Vaiśeṣika system for its drawing absolute distinctions between categories. When the distinction is asserted absolutely as does the Nyāya-Vaiśeṣika system, the fallacy of *naigamābhāsa* is committed.

Another interpretation of the *naigama naya* found in the Jaina tradition is that it relates to the end or the purpose of one or a series of actions. The illustration given in the *Tattvārthasāraḥ* is

[2] See C J Padmarajiah, *op. cit.*, p. 310

that of a person who carries water, rice and fuel, who when asked what he is doing replies: "I am cooking"[3] instead of saying "I am carrying fuel" and so forth. This means each one of the acts, viz., getting water, gathering fuel, etc., is controlled by a purpose or teleology, cooking food. At the time of the reply itself cooking is not done, but the purpose is very much present in every one of the series of acts necessary for 'achieving' it.

Saṅgraha Naya : (The Class Point of View)

The standpoint is concerned with the general properties or class-characteristics rather than with the specific qualities of the objects analysed. This does not mean that it is opposed to considering reality as a complex of the universal and particular, or considering it in its specific attributes. It signifies merely that a standpoint — a purely analytical one — can be taken from which the universal characteristic may be 'extracted' from the universal-particular complex. The principle underlying any classification is that there are some similarities binding the divergent individual or particular entities and the *saṅgraha naya* is especially concerned with the class-characteristics.

This *naya* should not be misinterpreted as containing a self-contradiction in Jaina thought. Having indicated, in an epistemological context that the particular without the universal as well as the universal without the particular are meaningless, it may be argued, the Jainas are now seen to argue out the case for the universal as against the particular. The seeming assertion of the universal here is attributable to the fact that under certain contexts, 'extracting' the one or the other is quite meaningful. That the Jainas were quite aware of the mistake is evident from their criticism of the Sāṅkhya and the Advaita schools for their committing the fallacy of *saṅgrahābhāsa*, the fallacy committed in over-emphasizing the universal aspect. The proposition "Everything is *sat*" is quite meaningful if it is not meant to deny the necessary complement of *asat* which is, at the time of uttering the universal proposition, 'shut out'.

[3] Cited in Y. J. Padmarajiah, *op. cit.* p. 314

Vyavahāra Naya : (The Standpoint of the Particular)

Unlike the *saṅgraha naya* the *vyavahāra naya* is concerned with the specific properties of an object without overlooking the fact that the specific qualities are not independently conceivable, i. e., without any reference at all to the generic qualities binding the various particulars. When for instance, we say "Reality as Substance possesses Existence and Modes" we have specific references to the nature of Substance itself. The point to be noted is that in the very act of specifying some properties possessed by Reality, Reality is implied as the substratum of the properties, i.e., the universal itself is not ignored when the particular is mentioned.

The fallacy of *vyavahāranayābhāsa* is committed when there is the assertion of the empirical at the cost of the universal. According to the Jaina view the Cārvākas committed this fallacy when they dwelt too much on the empirical — in the name of believing only that knowledge which they got through the sense organs.

The three *nayas* described above are a result of looking at the identity of things. In general, the three *nayas* are attempts at understanding the substance or *dravya* aspect of Reality. Hence they are referred to as *dravyārthika nayas.* The other four *nayas* yet to be described indicate the standpoints that are possible when we analyse Reality from the point of view of the modes possessed by it. Hence they are known as *paryāyārthika nayas.*

Ṛjusūtra Naya : (The Standpoint of Momentariness)

This standpoint considers only the present form of the object to be significant. It not merely does not consider the past and the future but considers that even the whole of the present is of no consequence. It extracts the mathematical present, the momentary state of existence of the object. The past is no more and the future is not yet and so, to refer to an object which is no longer present or is yet to come into existence is a sheer case of contradiction. We can be sure of only the present, the mathematical, the fleeting, the momentary present. The standpoint is illustrated by our treating an actor as a king on the stage when that role is played by him. To treat him as a king even outside the stage is not proper.

The 'extraction' of the present from the empirical, also termed 'concentrating on the occurrent aspect' again should not be 'overdone.' While recognizing the importance and the relative validity of this occurrent aspect in the life of Reality, we are not expected to lose sight of the continuant character of Reality.[4]

Śabda Naya : (The Standpoint of Synonymns)

The standpoint refers to the significance of the synonymous words we come across in any language. The synonymous words stand for certain meanings implied in the synonymns. The similarity in the meanings are discernible in spite of the dissimilarities observable in the tenses, case-endings, etc., of the words. We find two examples in the Jaina works to illustrate this *naya.* The words *kuṁbha*, *kalaśa* and *ghaṭa* refer to the same object, viz., the jar. Similarly the various names like Indra, Śakra and Purandara denote the one individual man. It is not asserted here that there is complete identity between the various synonymns or names. When, however, complete identity between two words is asserted, the fallacy of *śabdanayābhāsa* is committed.

Samabhirūḍha Naya : (The Etymological Standpoint)

In a sense this *naya* is just the reverse of the last one. This *naya* concentrates on the dissimilarities between words. Synonymns are no exception. Even words which are generally considered to be synonymns are found to be dissimilar when their etymology is studied. For example the term Indra stands for one who is 'all prosperous', Śakra stands for one who is 'all powerful' and Purandara stands for one who is a 'destroyer of enemies'. The difference we see in the root-meanings of the terms points to the actual differences between the terms and consequently to the differences in meanings or significance. According to an ancient Jaina thinker, rejection of this standpoint would entail an acceptance of non-difference between even non-synonymous words like *ghaṭa* (pot) and *paṭa* (cloth).

A Jaina scholar points out that the truth of this view-point is based on the following two principles in the Jaina philosophy of

[4] See C. J. Padmarajiah, *op. cit.*, p. 320

language : The first principle is that whatever is knowable is also expressible. That is, knowledge or the meaning of anything in reality, is not possible except through the means of words. The second principle is that, strictly speaking, there can be only one meaning and *vice versa*. Accordingly, several words which are conventionally supposed to convey one and the same meaning, have in actual fact as many meanings as the number of words found there. That is, this principle does not recognize any synonymous terms but maintains a determinate relation between a meaning and its word (*vācyavācakaniyama*).[5]

Evaṁbhūta Naya : (The 'Such-like' Standpoint)

This is a logical consequence of the etymological approach. In the etymological method we are concerned with the root from which the word itself is derived. The derivative significance is considered by the *evaṁbhūta naya* as pointing to the 'performance of an actual function' suggested by the etymology of the word. The meaning of the term *evaṁbhūta* is 'true in its entirety in the word and the sense'. In an example cited earlier, the individual can be referred to as Purandara only when he is actually destroying the enemies. Similarly, only when the individual is actually exhibiting his prowess can he be referred to as *Śakra*.

Each one of the *nayas* is considered to have one hundred subdivisions. Thus totally there are seven hundred *nayas*. We find two other views also expressed, — one maintaining that there are only six *nayas* and the other asserting that there are five *nayas* only. The first one accepts the six *nayas* other than the *naigama naya*, and the second one includes the *samabhirūḍha naya* and the *evaṁbhūta naya* in the *śabda naya*.

[5] *Ibid.*, pp. 322-23

24

Syadvada

THE most distinguishing feature of Jaina metaphysics is found reflected in the doctrine of 'may be' which asserts that no single proposition can express the whole of Reality fully. The term *syādvāda* is derived from the term *syāt* meaning 'may'. If the aim of metaphysical inquiry is to comprehend Reality, the Jainas point out, it cannot be achieved by formulating certain simple, categorical propositions merely. Reality being complex any one simple proposition cannot express the nature of Reality fully. That is the reason why the term 'May be' is appended to the various propositions concerning Reality by the Jaina philosophers. As will be evident from the sequel, seven propositions are put forward by the Jaina philosophers, without any affirmation whatsoever in regard to any one of the propositions. Dasgupta explains the significance of the term 'May be' as follows : "The truth of each affirmation is ... only conditional, and inconceivable from the absolute point of view. To guarantee correctness, therefore, each affirmation should be preceded by the phrase *syāt* ('may be'). This will indicate that the affirmation is only relative, made somehow, from some point of view and under some reservations and not in any sense absolute. There is no judgment which is absolutely true, and no judgment which is absolutely false. All judgments are true in some sense and false in another."[1]

The *nayavāda* of the Jainas provides the frame-work for the

[1] *op. cit.*, Vol. I, p. 179

syādvāda since it clearly points out that Reality can be looked at from many different standpoints, and that no standpoint can be claimed as the only valid one. It was on this ground that the Jainas accepted the truths in schools as different as the Cārvāka and Advaita while,at the same time, being critical of them and the others. The reason for the Jaina philosophers' accepting the truth contained in the divergent schools of thought was that from one particular standpoint what the rival schools said was right. The very same schools came to be criticised strongly by the Jainas for over-emphasizing a particular point of view, for rejecting, in effect, that there *can be* other points of view as well. In the doctrine of *syādvāda* we find the extension and application of the principle of *naya* to take a definite view of Reality, by means of seven propositions. That is why *syādvāda* is also referred to as *saptabhaṅgīnaya.*

That in *syādvāda* there is a definite view of Reality is quite often not understood at all by the critics of Jainism. The significance of having seven propositions is also not properly appreciated. Since we find the prefix 'may be' or 'perhaps' (*syāt*) in every proposition, the critics point out that there is a kind of scepticism involved in the whole of the Jaina view of Reality. Since there are seven propositions, none of them being pointed out emphatically to be the only correct one, the critics point an accusing finger at Jainism and maintain that the Jaina philosophers *themselves* do not have any view of Reality.

But it is not realized that the Jaina has a definite view of Reality, viz., that no definite view of Reality can be really taken. This is found reflected in the seven-fold predication (*saptabhaṅgīnaya*). These seven propositions together are considered to give us an insight into the nature of Reality. Logically, a proposition stands for some idea or view, and when judgments are made about Reality and propositions formulated, they are believed to indicate aspects of Reality. The Jaina position that no definite view of Reality is possible signifies, therefore, that no one judgment can fully comprehend Reality and naturally that no one proposition is adequate to describe what is extremely complex and manifold (*anekānta*).

From what we have stated about the significance of *syādvāda* in general it is obvious that it complements the *nayavāda*. Whereas the emphasis in *nayavāda* is on an *analytical* approach to Reality, on pointing out that different standpoints can be taken, the stress in *syādvāda* is on the *synthetic* approach to Reality, on reiterating that the different view-points together help us in comprehending the Real. As analysis and synthesis are not unrelated to each other we find elements of synthesis even in a purely analytical approach and elements of analysis even in a synthetic view of Reality. In more concrete terms : in *nayavāda* there is the recognition that over-emphasizing any one view would lead to a fallacy—implying that the different views have their value, that each one of them reflects Reality and therefore, that they together alone can give us a sweep into Reality. Similarly in *syādvāda* the synthetic character of the modes of predication is highlighted with a clear understanding that various propositions synthesised have, each one of them, something to convey about Reality itself.

We shall now consider the seven propositions in some detail. The seven modes of predication are :

1. May be, Reality is (*Syāt asti dravyaṁ*)
2. May be, Reality is not (*Syāt nāsti dravyaṁ*)
3. May be, Reality is and is not (*Syāt asti ca nāsti ca dravyaṁ*)
4. May be, Reality is indescribable (*Syāt avaktavyaṁ dravyaṁ*)
5. May be, Reality is and is indescribable (*Syāt asti ca avaktavyaṁ dravyaṁ*)
6. May be, Reality is not and is indescribable (*Syāt nāsti ca avaktavyaṁ dravyaṁ*)
7. May be, Reality is, is not and is indescribable (*Syāt asti ca nāsti ca avaktavyaṁ dravyaṁ*)

As any object in the world represents Reality (though in a limited way), we shall explain the seven propositions with reference to a particular object, we shall take the example of a pot (*ghaṭa*) as the Jaina philosophers do. Before taking the propositions themselves for analysis it is important to remember that the terms *is* and *is not* stand respectively for the existence or otherwise of the object under consideration.

1. The proposition "May be Pot is" signifies obviously the existence of the pot. The prefixing of 'May be' to the proposition implies that this proposition is not absolutely true, i. e., in exclusion of the truth of all the other propositions. The proposition is valid from one point of view, that is from the point of view of the

presence of a particular factor. The Jaina philosophers refer to four main factors in this connection, the factors, namely of Substance (*dravya*), Place (*kṣetra*), Time (*kāla*) and Mode (*paryāya*). In regard to the pot, for example, it might be made of mud or any other substance. When we look at the pot from the point of view of the substance, mud : if it is made of mud, and only if it is made of mud we can assert the existence of the pot, not otherwise. Similarly the existence of the pot can be asserted from the point of view of its existence at a particular place, not from the point of view of the place where it is not. The other two factors may be similarly explained. The existence of the pot is true only from the point of view of the 'present', i. e., from the point of view of its presence during a particular period of time. The pot *was not* before its production and *will not be* after its destruction. From these points of view the existence of the pot cannot be maintained. Similarly when the mud, the basic substance is moulded in a particular way, and given a particular shape, we may say "the pot is", not otherwise. If given a different shape it exists in a different *mode* not in the mode we assert.

2. The proposition "Pot is not"—is not a contradictory of the first proposition. Only beween contradictory propositions we have absolute opposition, so that when we assert the truth of one (proposition) the falsity of the other is asserted and *vice versa.* Very often the opposition between the first and the second propositions is considered to be of the contradictory type and hence it is maintained that to say that the propositions "The pot exists" and "The pot does not exist" are both true is unintelligible and illogical. The implication is that if the pot exists its existence *cannot be denied* and if it does not exist, its existence *cannot be asserted.*

What is denied in the second proposition is not the existence of the pot as far as the specific qualities asserted are concerned. There is the act of denial only when other properties which are not positively present are asserted. In more concrete terms : the proposition "The pot does not exist" does not signify "The pot does not exist as pot". It means merely that the pot does not exist as cloth (*paṭa*) or as anything else.

3 & 4. The third and the fourth propositions, viz., "The Pot is and is not" and "The pot is indescribable"—clearly point to the Jaina view that Reality as also the objects that reflect it are com-

plex in nature, so that looked at from the point of view of the presence of all the different attributes that constitute it we may speak meaningfully of the presentation of the togetherness of the attributes. In regard to the two attributes, in the example, of the existence and the non-existence of the pot : the third and the fourth propositions embody different ways of presenting the togetherness of the two modes, existence and non-existence.

In the third proposition there is the successive presentation of the two modes. In the proposition "The pot is and is not" the first part is true from the point of view of the existence of the individual property of the pot, in this case the 'property' of existence. The second part of the proposition "is not" is true from the point of view of the non-existence of other properties. The two propositions constituting the complex third proposition, if successively asserted contain a definite description of Reality. It is hence said that in the third proposition there is a consequitive presentation of the two or that a 'differenced togetherness' of two properties is asserted.

The fourth proposition "The pot is indescribable" is born out of a realization that simultaneous attention to both aspects of it is a psychological and a logical impossibility. Existence and non-existence, being mutually exclusive cannot be simultaneously attributed to one and the same thing. Therefore when the existence aspect as well as the non-existence aspect are simultaneously asserted the object is not described at all. Hence it is said that the object is indescribable. The simultaneous presentation of the two modes is referred to also as 'co-presentation' and as 'differenced togetherness' of the attributes.

After discussing the first four propositions, M. Hiriyanna observes : "It may seem that the formula might stop here. But there are still other ways in which the alternatives can be combined. To avoid the impression that those predicates are excluded, three more steps are added. The resulting description becomes exhaustive, leaving no room for the charge of dogma in any form."[2]

5. The fifth proposition "The Pot is and is indescribable" points to the fact that looked at from the point of view of the existent form the pot is describable but if both its existent and non-

[2] *Outlines of Indian Philosophy* (London : George Allen and Unwin Ltd., 1957), p. 165

existent forms are considered simultaneously it becomes indescribable.

6. The sixth proposition "The Pot is not and is indescribable" like the fifth proposition asserts the describability as well as indescribability of the pot. Even the non-existence of the properties other than those which are actually present in the object do not make it indescribable, a negative description still being possible. If, however, the negative and positive descriptions are simultaneously attempted, we have the situation of indescribability.

7. The seventh proposition "The Pot is, is not and is indescribable" signifies that successive presentation of the two aspects, the positive and the negative—points to the describability whereas simultaneous presentation of them brings out our inability to give any description of the pot.

The seven propositions can be formulated in regard to the eternality and non-eternality, identity and difference, etc. of any object. The Jaina philosophers believe that the seven modes of predication together give us an adequate description of Reality.

We may conclude our discussion of the *syādvāda* theory by quoting Eliot who, in one sentence, has brought out the essential significance of the theory. He says : "The essence of the doctrine, so far as one can disentangle it from scholastic terminology, seems just, for it amounts to this, that as to matters of experience it is impossible to formulate the whole and complete truth, and as to matters which transcend experience, language is inadequate..."[3] Apart from the pains the Jaina philosophers have taken to describe Reality the doctrine brings out the humility of approach of the Jaina philosophers to philosophic problems.

[3] *op. cit.*, Vol. I, p. 108

PART V

ETHICS

25

The Ethical Code

WE have already made a reference to the five ethical principles prescribed by Mahāvīra to his followers : *ahiṁsā* (non-violence), *satya* (truth), *asteya* (non-stealing), *brahmacarya* (celibacy) and *aparigraha* (non-possession).

Of these five principles the first one is considered to be the most important. The most predominant characteristic of Jainism is its insistence on the strict observance of the principle of non-violence. The use of the negative prefix has been misunderstood and the result is that the positive philosophy of love contained in the ethics of non-violence is not appreciated fully. S. C. Thakur explains : "Even if 'complete absence of ill-will' does not *literally* mean a positive attitude of good will and love it comes very close to the latter. This. . . brings the essential presupposition of *ahiṁsā*, in spite of the use of a grammatically negative term, very much closer to a positive philosophy of love."[1] The deeper significance of the term can be appreciated from the fact that Jainism believing as it does in 'continuity of consciousness' (as explained previously in this work), considers that man has no right to interfere with the progress (spiritual) of *any* being—even of the one-sensed. Injury involved positive interference and so there was to be exhortation to practise non-interference.

The term is sometimes interpreted as strict non-killing. Though

1 *Christian and Hindu Ethics* (London : George Allen and Unwin Ltd., 1969), p. 202

both the terms—non-violence and non-killing—seem on the surface to connote a negative teaching without a positive content, on a deeper analysis we find that observing the principle faithfully entails a positive and all-comprehensive view of life. No wonder, therefore, the observance of the principle severely has also been criticised. Monier Williams, in his article on Jainism, for instance, mentions that the Jainas outdo every other Indian sect in carrying the prohibition of *hiṁsā* to the most preposterous extremes. The institution of pinjrapol, the hospital for diseased animals in Bombay has been cited as an example by him.[2] Mrs Stevenson takes the view that the ideal of non-violence is scientifically impossible for a life-motto, since it is contrary to the code of nature.[3] The two views mentioned here are due to the fact that the historical background of the concept is not known to many scholars. The polemic attitude of the Jainas against sacrificing innocent animals in the name of propitiating the gods and performing sacrifices (*yājñas*) is too well-known to need detailed analysis here. There was also a strong protest against injustice done to life in general. The protests of the Jainas (and the Bauddhas) against inflicting pain and taking life did make their impact on Indian ethics itself. The practical application of the principle by Mahatma Gandhi is only an extension of the traditional value of *ahiṁsā*. Gandhiji himself has stated that he derived much benefit from the Jaina religious works as from the scriptures of other great faiths of the world.[4]

Non-violence and non-killing are generally associated with 'acts' so that if the individual concerned does not indulge in the prohibited acts he is absolved of the sins that might accrue to him. But though the act itself has to be avoided, the intention also must be pure. Since an act is always preceded by an intention and a will, mere avoidance of the act may not necessarily mean that there was no intention. The intention might have been there, but with great difficulty the act itself might have been avoided. What is insisted upon by the Jaina philosophers is that the mind (*manas*) must be completely free from evil intentions—here meaning intention to kill or commit violence. In the *Tattvārtha-Sūtra* we read

[2] Cited in T. G. Kalghatgi, *Jaina View of Life* (Sholapur : Jaina Saṁskriti Saṁrakshaka Saṅgha, 1969), p. 163

[3] *op. cit.*, p. 287

[4] See *The Letter from Gandhiji* in the Modern Review, Oct. 1916

that *hiṁsā* is injury or violence caused to the living organism due to carelessness and negligence, and actuated by passions like pride, prejudice, attachment and hatred.[5] It is clear, the physical act was not considered in isolation from the mental attitude. The importance of *manas* is emphasized in another Jaina classic thus : "Negligence brings sin; and the soul is defiled even though there may not be any actual injury to life. On the contrary, a careful and a pious person who is not disturbed by passions and who is kind towards animals will not suffer the sin of violence, even if, by accident, injury is caused to life."[6]

Co-ordination between the mind and body is thus considered necessary for the practice of non-violence. This should be accompanied also by proper speech emanating from the heart which knows nothing but love. The result is that there is absolutely no thought of injury and no speech of it either—indicating that there is no instigation of somebody else to commit violence. Hence the principle of *ahiṁsā* naturally implies purity of thought, word and deed and is a result of universal love and sympathy towards all living beings, however low they may be in the scale of evolution. Eliot exhibits a clear understanding of the Jaina view of non-violence when he writes : ". . . the beautiful precept of *ahiṁsā* or not injuring living things is not, as Europeans imagine, founded on the fear of eating one's grandparents but rather on the humane and enlightening feeling that all life is one and that men who devour beasts are not much above the level of the beasts who devour one another."[7]

In the observance of the principle of non-violence the householder is given some concession, allowed some laxity; the ascetic, however, is expected to follow the principle to its minutest detail. For example, in regard to the killing of the one-sensed living organisms found in the vegetables, the ascetic is allowed no concession. The house-holder is allowed to kill the one-sensed organism, since, in the absence of it, agriculture as an avocation will suffer and consequently society will be deprived of a basic necessity of life, viz., food. The house-holder is therefore expected to observe this principle only in regard to the two-sensed, three-sensed, four-sensed

5 *Tattvārtha-Sūtra*, VII. 8

6 *Pravacanasāra*, III. 17

7 *op. cit.*, Vol. I, p. lvi

and five-sensed living organisms. The stricter adherence prescribed for the ascetic is known as the *mahāvrata* and the less scrupulous observance expected of a house-holder is referred to as *aṇuvrata*.

The Jainas were extremely critical of the Buddhists' being allowed to eat meat on the ground that they themselves did not kill the animals but that they were getting the meat from the butchers. The Jaina view is that but for the meat-eaters the butchers themselves would not indulge in the evil act of killing the animals and that such meat-eaters are responsible (though indirectly) for killing. The Jainas were equally critical of the Hindu practice of sacrificing animals in their ritualistic observance on the ground that sacrifices involving deliberate killing of animals was an unethical act, though done in the name of religion.

Satya : (Truth-speaking)

This is the second virtue to be practised by all people. In the case of the house-holder the strict observance of the principle is not insisted. The spirit of the principle is all that needs to be followed.[8] *Ahiṁsā* or non-violence being the most important virtue to be followed, all other virtues are to be observed in such a way that the principle of non-violence is not broken. In a situation where truth-speaking would lead to violence or killing, as for example revealing the place in which a man is hiding (to escape from the robbers who are intent on killing), uttering falsehood deliberately is considered perfectly ethical. In this case the outcome of uttering lying speech is the avoidance of killing and, as such it is preferable to speaking the truth and becoming instrumental to violence or killing. Similarly when an animal is hiding under a bush which the hunter has not noticed, the individual is not expected to reveal the truth lest the animal should be killed.

[8] The Jaina philosophers were very much alive to the fact that in his every day life the house-holder cannot avoid all words which will hurt--and 'entangle' him and so cannot avoid *asutya*....especially in regard to his house-hold, profession and security of life. So exceptions were made in regard to these and avoidance of falsehood in regard to all other aspects was all that was advocated as constituting the essence of *satya*. Negatively truthfulness consisted in avoiding exaggeration, fault-finding and indecent speech; positively it consisted in speaking beneficial, balanced and noble words.

Asteya : (Non-stealing)

This virtue signified the strict adherence to one's own possessions, not even *wanting* to take hold of another's. All the evil practices observed in trade and commerce such as adulterating the materials and not giving others their money's worth, not weighing or measuring properly and indulging in black-marketing—constitute *Steya* or stealing. Carefully and scrupulously avoiding such malpractices constitutes the observance of the *asteya vrata*.

Once again in the matter of the observance of this *vrata* it is realized that the house-holder has his limitations. So the relative observance alone is expected of him. The observance, in the case of the house-holder consists in his not taking things which were not offered to him, not taking things which were placed or dropped or forgotten by others. Similarly he was to avoid purchasing things at cheaper prices if the cheaper price was due to an improper method employed in acquiring the object. Underground and unclaimed property belonged to the king and the house-holder was not to take them; if he found them, he was to promptly inform the king about it.

Brahmacarya : (Celibacy)

In the case of the ascetic this virtue signifies complete abstention from sex. Abstention is certainly in regard to the act, but even thoughts entertained about sex were considered to be undesirable and as bad and unethical as the sexual act itself. The principle of co-ordination of thought, word and deed is applicable to the principle of celibacy as well.

In the case of the house-holder, it is obvious, the principle cannot be understood in its literal and strict sense. Insistence on the strict adherence to abstention from sex would entail a contradiction in the very existence of a home and a family for the individual. The Jaina philosophers were not blind to this aspect of the problem. Hence they have suggested that in the case of the house-holder the observance of the principle, in spirit, is done by observing the principle of monogamy. Living a life of *brahmacarya* in the case of the house-holder signifies being completely faithful to one's wife (or husband) as the case may be. Even thinking of other women (or men) would be doing damage to the principle. Leading a strict monogamic life is synonymous with observing sex purity and it helps the individual in securing for himself and for others domestic happiness.

Aparigraha : (Non-possession)

This principle is obvious in the case of the ascetic since he has necessarily to reno unce all his property and wealth before taking to the 'Order'. But the mere physical renunciation is not of much value. He must also have no thoughts whatever of the things renounced. Because of their constant association with him, it is very likely that thoughts about his former possessions may still linger on in his mind. The ascetic has to combat the tendency to retrospect about what he no longer 'possesses'.

It will be seen from the above that though reference is mainly made to property or wealth, strictly speaking the principle is extendable to the cultivation of a particular type of attitude towards life. Man's attachments towards his home and people as well as so many other things relating to them becomes so much that it will not be an exaggeration to maintain that he considers them all as his 'possessions'. The true ascetic has to practise the quality of detachment to such an extent that he will consider everything including his body and mind as hindrances to his reaching the goal of life, *mokṣa*.

In the case of the house-holder non-possession signifies putting a stop to his desires for more than his just. The idea behind the Jaina philosophers' liberal attitude towards the house-holders in regard to the practice of the virtue is that a strict adherence to the principle would be detrimental to society as a whole. Whatever might be the profession, the application of the principle entails an honest, and not merely an efficient performance of the duties. In the case of the trader, for example, efficiency would entail a proper understanding and application of business principles so as to facilitate the augmentation of the economic resources. Honesty on the part of the trader means, scrupulousness in the matter of considering his profession as a means to his individual happiness and also social welfare and not as an end-in-itself. By adopting the right or ethical methods in his profession he will be helping his society to derive the maximum benefit out of his skill in producing wealth.

The detached outlook toward life as a whole which man is to ultimately adopt is thus practised even while leading an ordinary house-holder's life. Ultimately man is to curb all his desires and attain purity of self. In the matter of cultivating a sense of detachment in every-day life the principle of non-possession thus means imposing a voluntary limitation on his desires. The principle as observable by the house-holder is referred to as *parimitaparigraha.*

The five ethical principles are thus the guide-posts for man who is in search of his own self. The integrated pattern observable in the ethical principles is evident from the fact that all the principles are ultimately to be referred to the standard of non-violence. The observance of the integrated ethical scheme, the Jainas believe, helps man in the matter of realizing personality-integration.

26

Doctrine of Karma

ALL the Indian systems of philosophy except the Cārvāka school accept the theory of *karma*. By and large the theory of *karma* is brought in as a causal law to explain various phenomena in human life. The precise meaning given to the term *karma* differs from school to school. For our purposes here we need concern ourselves only with a point of contrast between the schools of Hindu philosophy that accept the concept of *karma* and the Jaina system. The other systems of Indian thought understand *karma* to stand for action, though the term *action* itself is given different interpretations by the various schools constituting the group. The Jaina philosophers give a strictly materialistic interpretation to the term *karma*. *Karma*, according to the Jaina philosophers, signifies an aggregate of extremely fine matter which is imperceptible to the senses.

The argument put forward by the Jaina philosophers to maintain the material nature of *karma* is interesting. It is held that an effect having a material form must have had a material cause. The atoms constituting the real objects in the universe, for example, may be considered to be the 'causes' of the objects, and, the atoms being considered material, the causes of objects also ought to be considered material. An initial objection against this fundamental position anticipated by the Jainas is that experiences like pleasure, pain, enjoyment and suffering are purely mental and therefore their causes also must be mental, i. e., non-material. *Karma* cannot hence be brought in to account for these human experiences. The Jaina's reply is that these experiences are not wholly independent of corporeal causes, since the experiences of pleasure, pain, etc. are associated with for example, food, etc. There is no experience of pleasure etc., in association with a non-material entity, just as in connection with the ether.[1] It is thus maintained that at the back of these experiences there are 'natural causes' and that is *karma.* It is in this sense that *karma* is responsible for all human experiences, enjoyable and otherwise, desirable as well as undesirable, etc.

Since the strict dualism of Jainism admits of the entities *jīva* and *ajīva,* the non-material and the material or the spiritual and the non-spiritual principles, holding *karma* responsible for *all experiences,* signifies : (i) that the experiences are of the *jīva* which alone possesses consciousness ; (ii) that the experiences themselves are due to the union, combination or mixing up of the two principles and (iii) that when there are no experiences, no limitations are imposed on the *jīva.* The Jaina philosophers argue that from our experiences it cannot but be concluded that the kārmic matter has mixed up with the pure soul and imposes limitations on the purity of consciousness which is the intrinsic nature of *jīva.* Under the evil influence of *karma,* the soul which is pure and unlimited in its capacities *feels* it is 'limited'. The 'release' of the soul from the negative influence of *karma* is the *sine qua non* for liberation or *mokṣa,* the ultimate goal in life to be reached.

The binding of the *jīva* itself takes place through two types of *karma,* the physical and the psychical. The first type signifies the influx of matter into the soul and the second type stands for the various conscious activities (mental) such as likes and dislikes. The two types of *karma* are considered to be responsible 'highly' for each other.

The *karma* particles, it is held, bind men for varying lengths of time. It is because of this that the lengths of experiences, both good and bad also vary. It is important to notice that whatever might be the length of time during which the *karma* particles affect the *jīva,* the Jainas firmly believe that the *jīva* can free itself from the shackles of *karma.* The time-factor referred to here is designated the *duration* of *karma.*

The *karmas* affecting the soul also depend on the intensity of

1 *Karma-grantha,* I. 3

the passions and actions involved. The more deeply the person is involved, the more attachment the person has, the stronger is the binding power of *karma*. Similarly, depending on the strength of the action, there is either mild or strong experience of the effect of *karma*. This aspect of *karma* is referred to as the *intensity* of *karma*.

The material conception of *karma* naturally entails the quantity of *karma* affecting the *jīva* at a given time. Since the *karma* particles are believed to infect the soul, it is held by the Jaina philosophers that the soul attracts the *karma* particles just lying outside it. The attraction depends on the activity of the self. The more intensive the activity of the self, the more is the quantity of *karma* attracted by it. Conversely, the less the intensity of the activity of the self, the less is the quantity of the kārmic particles attracted by the soul. It is from this point of view that it is said that renunciation of activity helps the self to get release or *mokṣa*. Since, however, it is held that there is bondage only because of 'passions', it is pointed out that if actions are performed without passions they do not bind the individual. The third aspect of the *karma* theory we have just now considered is the *quantitative aspect*.

The fourth aspect refers to the *nature* of *karma* as constituting eight types and encompassing one hundred and fifty eight sub-species. The eight main types are : Comprehension-obscuring (*jñānāvaraṇa*), apprehension-obscuring (*darśanāvaraṇa*), feeling-producing (*vedanīya*), deluding (*mohanīya*), age-determining (*āyus*), personality-making (*nāma*), status-determining (*gotra*) and power-obscuring (*antarāya*). Of these, the first four are the obstructive (*ghātin*) and the rest are the non-obstructive (*aghātin*) type. We shall now indicate the various sub-species of the different types of *karma*.

Jñānāvaraṇa : Since knowledge is of five types, we have, corresponding to them five types of knowledge-obscuring *karmas* according as they obscure *mati, śruta, avadhi, manaḥparyāya* or *kevalajñāna*.[2]

Darśanāvaraṇa : This is of nine kinds. The first four correspond to the four types of *darśana* and the rest, to the five kinds of sleep.[3]

[2] *Ibid.*, I. 4-9
[3] *Ibid.*, I. 10-12

The first type obscures vision and is referred to as *cakṣurdarśanāvaraṇa karma*. The next one obscures the non-visual apprehension and is known as *acakṣurdarśanāvaraṇa karma*. The next two varieties respectively obscure clairvoyance and omniscience and go by the name of *avadhi-darśanāvaraṇa karma* and *kevala-darśanāvaraṇa karma*. The next five are concerned respectively with producing light sleep, deep sleep, sleep while still the person is sitting or standing, sleep while walking and somnambulism. These are the *nidrā-vedanīya, nidrā-nidrā-vedanīya, pracalā-vedanīya, pracalā-pracalā-vedanīya* and *styāna-gṛddhi-vedanīya karmas*.

Vedanīyā : This is of two types—that which produces the feelings of pleasure (*sātāvedanīya* or *sadvedya*) and that which is responsible for the feeling of pain (*asātāvedanīya* or *asadvedya*).[4]

Mohanīya : This is of twenty-eight kinds.[5] The general classification is into the *darśana-mohanīya* and the *cāritra-mohanīya*, respectively concerned with obscuring right vision and right conduct. The first one is sub-divided into three and the second, into twenty-five.

Āyus : This is sub-divided into four and they are concerned with the determination of the duration of life (longevity) in the four states of the *jīva*, viz., the celestial, the human, the animal and the hell-being. Hence these are referred to as *deva-āyus-karma, manuṣya-āyus-karma, tiryag-āyus-karma* and *naraka-āyus-karma*.[6]

Nāma : This is considered to be of one hundred and three types. These are mostly quoted in a fixed succession in four groups: collective types (*pindaprakṛtis*) consisting of seventy-five sub-species, individual types (*pratyeya-prakṛtis*) consisting of eight sub-species, ten types of self-movable body (*trasa daśaka*) and ten types of immovable body (*sthāvara daśaka*).[7] Some examples in regard to the four types may be noted here. Firmness of joints, symmetry (or otherwise) of the body and complexion of the individual—these are some examples for the first type. The individual's having a feeling of superiority, his capability to found a Holy Order, etc. are some of the examples for the second type. The individual having a handsome (or beautiful, as the case may be) body, posses-

4 *Ibid.*, I. 12

5 *Ibid.*, I. 14-22

6 *Ibid.*, I. 23

7 Glasennap, *op. cit.*, p. 11

sing a sweet voice and having a sympathetic disposition—these are all due to the third type. The individual looking ugly, possessing an unsympathetic disposition and a harsh voice—these are all due to the fourth type.

Gotra : This concerns the type of family in which the individual is born. Accordingly it is of two types—that which is responsible for the favourable and high family surroundings and that which makes the individual being born in a family in which there is no congenial atmosphere.[8]

Antarāya : This is of five types and is responsible for obscuring the inherent power of the soul. The five types obscure respectively charity, profit-making, enjoyment, circumstances under which enjoyment will be possible and will-power. These are referred to as *dāna-antarāya*, *lābha-antarāya*, *upabhoga-antarāya* and *vīrya-antarāya karmas.*[9]

In conclusion it should be noted that the individual himself is responsible for these various types of *karmas* and that these are not imposed on him from without. As such the responsibility of the individual is asserted and there is no suggestion even, of fatalism. Specific mention of the various types of *karma* responsible for the physical aspect of the individual suggests clearly that if the individual himself is responsible in determining the physical side of his being, it is very much more the case when it comes to determining the psychic and the spiritual aspects. The *karma* theory of the Jainas thus points to the fact that the individual is responsible for his own fate.

8 *Karma-grantha*, I. 52

9 *Ibid*

The Ethical Categories

IT is well-known that the metaphysical categories of any philosophical system are closely related to the system of ethics propounded, especially if it is considered that there is a 'higher ethic'. Oftentimes the term 'metaphysical roots of ethics' is made use of to describe the situation of mutual involvement of the metaphysical and the ethical categories. In Jainism also we find the ethical categories separately being mentioned and treated in detail. Nine ethical categories are accepted and these are : *jīva* (the conscious principle), *ajīva* (the non-conscious principle), *puṇya* (virtuous deed), *pāpa* (vicious deed), *āśrava* (influx of kārmic particles), *bandha* (bondage due to *karma*), *saṁvara* (prevention of the influx of *karma*), *nirjara* (partial annihilation of *karma*) and *mokṣa* (liberation or total annihilation of *karma*).

The close correlation between the metaphysical and the ethical categories is obvious. We find *jīva* and *ajīva*, the metaphysical categories being mentioned under the ethical categories also. While discussing *jīva* and *ajīva* as metaphysical categories we have made clear the Jaina view that *saṁsāra* or life-cycle is ultimately due to these two categories coming together, getting mixed up and giving the impression that there is no end at all to the cycle of birth and death. Though it was stated that these two eternal and independent principles come together as a result of which purity of consciousness is lost, we have not described the mechanics of the change that comes about by means of which the independent status of the *jīva* is lost. Similarly we have also not indicated how the purity of consciousness which was lost, thanks to the impact of *ajīva* on *jīva,* can be regained. In their treatment of the ethical categories the Jaina philosophers have systematically dealt with these two questions, viz., the way in which the self which is free gets bound and the way it gets back its lost freedom. Since we have already dealt with *jīva* and *ajīva* we need confine ourselves to an analysis of the other seven principles (*tattvas*).

Puṇya and *Pāpa* : These are considered to be the results respectively of good and bad deeds, virtuous and vicious conduct. From the point of view of the man who is suffering, no doubt, the man who is 'enjoying' is better off. But, from an ultimate point of view it is held that the condition of the one is not better than the other since both of them are still in the cycle of life and death. The condition of both men is traced by the Jaina philosopher to deeds done previously—not necessarily to the just previous life.[1] So, if the man who is suffering is to have more enjoyable experiences he should stop leading an ethically bad life and start treading on the path of a virtuous life. It is obvious that even the performance of good deeds is not effective in the matter of securing freedom or liberation (*mokṣa*) for the individual. Since freedom signifies an escape from the cycle of birth and death altogether, it necessarily means that it transcends both virtue and vice. That is, the liberated man is beyond good and evil. Since the good as well as the bad deeds imply a pre-disposition to do them, since they signify that there is a positive liking to do either of them, it is stated that the good as well as the bad *karmas* have a shackling effect on the *jīva*, and hence limit its freedom.

Examples of good actions are : acquiring right faith (*samyag-darśana*) and right knowledge (*samyagjñāna*), having reverential attitude towards great sages and observance of the various vows (*vrata*). The result of all these consists in the individual experiencing the feeling of pleasure (*sāta vedanīya*), leading an auspicious life (*śubha- āyus*), having a good physique (*śubhā-nāman*) and being born under favourable circumstances (*śubha-gotra*).[2] Having wrong faith, acquiring wrong knowledge, being violent, speaking falsehood, being sensuous, and entertaining attachments—in short, acts result-

[1] This has already been explained in Chapter 18.

[2] *Tattvārtha-Sūtra*, VIII. 25

ing from the non-observance of the five cardinal virtues—constitute bad actions. These result in the individual suffering the experience of pain (*asāta-vedanīya*), leading an evil life (*aśubha-āyus*), having an unattractive and unhealthy physique (*aśubha-nāman*) and being born amidst unfavourable surroundings (*aśubha-gotra*).[3]

Hence it is held by the Jaina philosophers that though leading a righteous life is better than leading an unrighteous one, it is not sufficient. No doubt, being born under favourable circumstances, having a healthy and long life, etc. facilitate the process of attaining perfection in that the chances of concentrating on the real problem of existence—problem of disengaging the *jīva* from the pollutions of the *ajīva*—become more. Here it should be noted that from the point of view of man himself we may say that the human ideal (of attaining liberation) gets more and more thought about as a result of favourable circumstances, but that the basic truth in Jainism is that freedom is not merely the ideal of man but that of the conscious principle (*jīva*) as a whole.

The ultimate ideal, being therefore the dissociation of the *jīva* from the *ajīva*, it cannot be attained merely by having pleasant experiences—however desirable these may be from the point of view of those who do not have them. The positive suggestion, therefore, is that since attachment is the ultimate cause of both good and bad actions and since both types of actions keep the individual 'bound', i. e., subjected to taking endless number of births to have the corresponding fruits, the aspirant for spiritual perfection should aim at developing the attitude of non-attachment. Once this happens, he is certainly on the highway leading to liberation. In respect of this suggestion Jainism does not differ from the other schools of Indian thought that escaping from the evils of *saṁsāra* entails an attitude of non-attachment towards both good and evil.

Āśrava and *Bandha* : The description of the next five categories is as interesting as it is important since it contains the clear-cut ideas of the Jaina philosophers on the way in which freedom from the evil effects of *karma* is obtained. It may not be out of place here to suggest that the Jaina description of the process of getting bound (by the *jīva*) and the 'technique' of liberation is almost along the lines on which the affliction of the physical body

[3] *Ibid.*, VIII. 26

by some malady and the way in which the body is freed of the malady is described in medicine.

The human body is considered in its natural state to possess resistance to the various types of diseases. But due to so many factors the body sometimes loses its resistance. This facilitates the various kinds of germs getting into the body and affecting it. The cure consists in the organism developing resistance and stopping the inflow of the disease-producing germs and also in positively getting rid of the germs which have already entered the body (or by making them ineffective). The parallellism will presently become evident.

The *jīva* which is pure in nature gets infected with the kārmic particles because of its psychical states of attachment, aversion, etc. Before the soul is actually affected by the kārmic particles there is the modification of the soul. We may well describe it as the soul losing its resistance to the 'infection' of *karma* and becoming susceptible to its evil influence. The first is referred to as *dravyāśrava* and the second, as *bhāvāśrava.* Since the modification of the soul precedes the soul getting polluted, nay, prepares the way to it, the ultimate cause of bondage is considered to be *bhāvāśrava* and not *dravyāśrava.* Impure psychic dispositions result from the lack of true faith, absence of discipline and having emotions like anger, jealousy, greed, etc. This aids the inflow of the kārmic particles towards the soul and the process of pollution. We also find a slightly different opinion in regard to the distinction we were referring to just now. In the place of the two types of *āśravas* we find acceptance of the principle of *āśrava* alone. *Āśrava* is defined as action of body, speech and mind.[4] It is obvious that though the psychical and physical actors have been clubbed together the spirit of the argument regarding the inflow of *karma* is the same. The vibratory activity of the soul caused by the body, mind and speech is technically called *yoga* and it is the most comprehensive cause of *āśrava* since it embraces both the empirical souls and the *Arhantas* within its range.[5] The *Siddhas* are beyond its range since they have no activity of the body, mind and speech.

Bandha is again due to *yoga*, but not *yoga* alone. The malig-

[4] *Ibid.*, VI. 1-2

[5] K. C. Sogani, *op. cit.*, p. 47

nant influence of passion in addition to the *yogas* are the causes of *bandha*. *Yoga* aided by passions attract fresh particles of *karma* and these get transformed into particles of *karma* and binds the *jīva*.

In regard to *bandha* also two stages are discernible, the *bhāva bandha* stage and the *dravya bandha* stage. Passions (*kaṣāyas*) like anger and pride stir consciousness and *karmas* create a peculiar kind of bondage known as *bhāva bandha*.[6] After this there is the actual contact of the kārmic particles with *jīva* and this results in *dravya bandha*.

Bandha is considered to be of four kinds : *prakṛti--bandha* (type-bondage), *pradeśa-bandha* (space-bonda e), *sthiti-bandha* (duration-bondage) and *anubhāga-bandha* (intensity of fruition bondage). Of these the first is the result of transformation of matter into kārmic particles due to the vibratory activity of the soul. It is mainly of eight types and these have been considered already. The *pradeśa-bandha* is logically the next type of *bandha* to be considered. Once there is the affection of the *jīva* by the various types of *karma*, karma-particles occupy the various space-points (*pradeśas*) of the soul—virtually making it impossible for the soul to escape from the clutches of *karma*. This type of bondage as well as the previous type are due to *yoga*[7] The third type, the *sthiti-bandha* refers to the fact that there is an incessant inflow of the kārmic particles and that there is a definite time-duration for the defilement to take place. As a result of the continuous flow of kārmic particles the kārmic particles get the potency to fructify and this results in the various types of experiences that the *jīva* has. The differences in the intensity of the experiences are due to the differences in their potencies created due to the different 'time-intervals' that lapse...This is the significance of the last type of *bandha*. The third and the fourth types are considered to result from passions.[8]

Saṁvara : This is the process of reversing the flow of the kārmic particles to effectively prevent the pollution of the soul.[9] Like the process of *āśrava*, *saṁvara* is also considered to be of two

6 *Tattvārtha-Sūtra*, VIII. 2-3
7 *Sarvārthasiddhi*, VIII. 3
8 *Ibid*
9 *Tattvārtha-Sūtra*, IX. 1

types : *bhāva-saṁvara* and *dravya-saṁvara*. The susceptibility to kārmic inflow is first checked. This is *bhāva-saṁvara*. In the absence of the root-cause of the flow of kārmic particles, the actual flow of kārmic particles is also not possible. This state of the stoppage of kārmic material is referred to as *dravya-saṁvara*.

Discriminative knowledge is the pre-requisite of *saṁvara*. In our context the term discriminative knowledge means the type of knowledge which unambiguously spells out the exact nature of the *jīva* and the *ajīva*. Whereas the intrinsic nature of the *jīva* is one of pure consciousness as long as knowledge proper does not dawn, purity of consciousness is not recognized. The various passions that the *jīva* has and the affections it is subjected to are not intrinsic to its character. Whereas they are considered to constitute the essential nature of the soul, they are, really speaking, only accidental to it. They can therefore be done away with without causing any damage to the soul. Again the various types of *karmas* with which the soul identifies itself are not as important as they seem to be in understanding the nature of the soul. In short, due to wrong knowledge, things which are distinct (*jīva* and *ajīva*) are not recognized to be so. The moment the recognition of the distinction between the two takes place, the soul gets freed from the delusions it was subjected to previously and it apprehends its own nature properly. The result of the 'self-apprehension' is that the various psychic states which result from ignorance are vitiated. This is *bhāva-saṁvara* proper and it paves the way to *dravya-saṁvara*. The flow of kārmic particles is stopped completely because of the absence of the psychic conditions which once facilitated it.

The *Dravyasaṅgraha* refers to seven varieties of *saṁvara vrata* (vow), *samiti* (carefulness), *gupti* (restraint), *dharma* (observance), *anuprekṣa* (meditation), *pariṣāhasaya* (victory over troubles) and *cāritra* (conduct). The *Tattvārtha-Sūtra* replaces *vrata* by *tapas* (penance).[10]

Nirjara : Two stages are recognized in the shedding of the *karmas*. The first stage refers to the modifications caused in the soul as a consequence of which partial disappearance of the kārmic particles results. This is *bhāva-nirjara*. The complete disappearance of the kārmic particles is the next stage known as *dravya-nirjara*.

[10] *Ibid.*, IX. 3

By hypothesis, the soul in this stage is possessed of discriminative knowledge and so even though the experiences (resulting from the fruition of *karma*) may be the same as in the pre-discriminative knowledge stage, in the *attitude* towards the experiences themselves we find a marked change. The change of attitude facilitates the shedding of *karmas*.

In the case of the one who is not possessed of the discriminative knowledge the various types of *karmas* he has indulged in previously set about various types of reactions in him (of course this is in addition to subjecting him to various types of experiences.) The reactions are because of the positive type of attachment he has towards enjoyable experiences and the negative attitude he has towards painful experiences. Not knowing that his various experiences are all due to his own previous actions with attachments and aversions, he identifies himself with them and is prone to be swept off his feet once again, thus entangling himself more and more in the vicious cycle of birth and death. On the other hand the person with the discriminative knowledge knows that his various experiences are not really intrinsic to his soul and so he has an attitude of detachment towards them. So whether he enjoys or suffers he remains unaffected. By adopting this attitude towards everything external to himself he allows the *karmas* to fructify, i. e., he exhausts the *karmas* he has already accumulated. Thus, by having experiences corresponding to his good and bad *karmas* but without getting affected in any way, the accumulated *karmas* are exhausted. We also find the view that through penances before the actual fructification of the *karmas* the *karmas* themselves are destroyed and made ineffective.

We may point out here that this aspect of the Jaina theory of *karma* presents an exact parallel to the Hindu theory according to which the *sañcita karma* even can be made ineffective by acquiring *jñāna*. The Hindu tradition also recommends to the spiritual aspirant the development of the attitude of non-attachment towards the *prārabdha-karma* so that getting involved further in the kārmic cycle can be avoided.

Mokṣa : Since we have already explained the *karma* theory and also the eight ethical categories, little remains to be added by way of elucidating the concept of *mokṣa*. *Mokṣa* is liberation—freeing of the *jīva* from the *ajīva*. The specific details regarding the disengagement of the *jīva* from the *ajīva* having been discussed, only a general reference need be made in regard to what is referred to as the three jewels (*tri-ratna*) of Jaina ethics, viz., *samyagdarśana*, *samyagjñāna* and *samyagcāritra*. The *tri-ratna* concept contains in it the quientessence of the Jaina theory of *mokṣa*.

Samyagdarśana is considered to be the prime cause of *mokṣa* inasmuch as it paves the way to right knowledge and right conduct. The *Yaśastilaka* tells us that "it is the prime cause of salvation, just as the foundation is the mainstay of a palace, good luck that of beauty, life that of bodily enjoyment, royal power that of victory, culture that of nobility and policy that of Government."[11] The *Uttarādhyana-Sūtra* envisages that right knowledge remains unattainable in the absence of right belief and rightness of conduct is out of the question without right knowledge.[12] *Samyagdarśana* itself is defined as faith in the seven *tattvas*, viz., *jīva*, *ajīva*, *āśrava*, *bandha*, *saṁvara*, *nirjara* and *mokṣa*.[13] The Jaina argument is that a person who has faith in the seven *tattvas* (right faith) gains right knowledge —right in the spiritual sense and not merely in the epistemological sense. Right knowledge as spiritual knowledge enables the individual to appreciate the nature of the *jīva* in its proper perspective and this enables him to adopt the practical steps leading to *mokṣa*. This is right conduct (*samyagcāritra*). The integrated nature of the ethico-spiritual disciplines leading to liberation has been fully appreciated by the Jaina philosophers and this is evident from the *tri-ratna* concept. None of these—right faith, right knowledge or right conduct—can be pursued meaningfully and effectively in isolation from each other, for the spiritual principle to be realized in life is neither a pure theoretical abstraction nor an easy thing which could be 'practised' merely. So, faith, knowledge and practical ethical living—all these are considered to be important and significant in the matter of attaining self-realization. The Jainas however insist that in the absence of faith the other two do not work. This is quite understandable in view of the fact that modern psychology has clearly indicated that 'faith' has in it the key to any cure.

[11] Cited in K. C. Sogani, *op. cit.*, pp. 60-61
[12] 28-30
[13] *Tattvārtha-Sūtra*, I, 2; *Dravyasaṅgraha*, 41

If in regard to physical and mental ailments this principle is seen to be efficacious, the Jaina's suggestion that spiritual 'cure' also is possible only when there is the basic faith in the principles suggested cannot be considered either as a theoretical abstraction or as propagating a dogmatic attitude in the spiritual aspirants.

28

The Six-fold Monastic Order

JAINISM considers that preparation for attaining the ultimate goal in life should not be postponed to that stage of life where there is complete renunciation. It maintains that renunciation is not physical merely, but is primarily mental. Hence the preparation to lead an ultimately spiritual life begins early in life. This is responsible for the two-fold classification of duties– the *śrāvaka-dharma* (the house-holder's duties) and the *muni-dharma* (the duties of the ascetic). We have already indicated that concession is allowed to the *śravāka* in the matter of observing the various virtues. In the case of the *muni* the five virtues of *satya*, *ahiṁsā*, *asteya*, *brahma-carya* and *aparigraha* are insisted to be followed very strictly. No laxity is allowed in his case.

The ideal in life for the *muni* is to have complete control over his body, mind and speech, for, only by perfecting himself in this regard can he observe the five virtues strictly and scrupulously. The endeavour to attain this three-fold control over himself is known as *gupti*. The *Sarvārthasiddhi* defines *gupti* as the supreme cause by virtue of which the *jīva* is able to transcend birth and death.[1] In this process, observing moderation in regard to the physical side of his being is extremely helpful. Moderation must be observed in regard to walking, speaking, bodily wants, careful handling of objects and answering calls of nature. These are referred to as *īrya-samiti*, *bhāṣā-samiti*, *eṣaṇa-samiti*, *ādāna-nikṣepaṇa-samiti* and

[1] *Sarvārthasiddhi*, IX. 2

utsarga-samiti.[2] The idea behind the prescription of the *samitis* is that unless bodily control is gained, mental control cannot even be thought of. We shall not go into the details regarding the observance of the various virtues here. Our purpose here is to indicate merely that the stage of the *muni* is considered to be more advanced than that of the *śrāvaka*.

In terms of spiritual evolution,—institution-wise—we have five more belonging to the ascetic order. These are the stages of the *ācārya*, *upādhyāya*, *sādhu*, *arahanta* and the *siddha*. These five institutions together with the institution of the *muni* are referred to as the six-fold monastic order of Jainism. We shall briefly consider the five stages that are 'more developed' than the stage of the *muni*.

Ācārya : The *ācārya* is the teacher (*guru*) in the spiritual sense of the term. He enjoys the privilege of initiating people into the spiritual path. In this respect Jainism accepts the Hindu view that an *ācārya* or teacher is essential for initiation. The duty of the *ācārya*, accordingly is to guide moral and spiritual conduct of his 'wards'. He has the responsibility to detect the erring disciples and to re-establish them on the correct path. He is also responsible for the governance and regulation of the monks of the Order. He is expected to possess a thorough knowledge of the Jaina scriptures as also a knowledge of the various other religions prevailling. This aspect of the *ācārya's* 'requirements' is extremely significant. Far from dogmatically propounding certain doctrines he is also to make a thorough study of his own religion in the light of the truths enshrined in the various other religions prevailing.

Upādhyāya : He is empowered to giving discourses on various spiritual matters. Naturally he is expected to have a deep knowledge of the various scriptures on which he discourses. Though he is discoursing on matters spiritual he is not privileged to correct the erring people. From the fact that this power is given to the *ācārya* it is obvious, the *ācārya* is considered to be more spiritually evolved. The *upādhyāya* is not yet so much evolved as to correct the others. Perhaps by repeatedly delivering lectures on the scriptures he gets more and more into the spirit of the various doctrines propounded and thus becomes more qualified in setting

2 *Tattvārtha-Sūtra*, IX. 5

about the task of correcting the others.

Sādhu : He is a saint who observes scrupulously the various codes of conduct prescribed for attaining spirituality in life. Compared to the *upādhyāya,* he is more of an introvert-type. He is not expected to give any spiritual discourses. The insistence on practising the various virtues in his own individual life first signifies that before one becomes eligible to give discourses on matters spiritual, he should himself have undergone the prescribed course of ethical life. The continued observance of the ethical virtues offers a real insight into the nature of spiritual life which is recommended while discoursing. Thus before the saint launches on a career of conveying the message of the scriptures to the masses he is required to have a real conviction in them and towards this his continued practice of the virtues is helpful.

Arahanta : This is a stage markedly advanced over the previous ones inasmuch as traces of anger, pride, deceit, greed, attachment, hatred and ignorance are not perceivable in the aspirant. In view of this the practice of *ahiṁsā* has been perfected in this stage. The *arahanta's* spirituality is so intense and so pure that it is radiated all round. The mere sight of the *arahanta* is considered to have the potentiality to convert hundreds of people to the path of spirituality and to destroy sceptical and perverse attitude towards life. Hence it is said that the very presence of the *arhat* is supremely enlightening.

Arhats are of seven types, the *pañcakalyāṇadhārī, tīnakalyāṇadhārī, dokalyāṇadhārī, sāmānyakevalī, sātiśayakevalī, upasargakevalī* and *antakṛtkevalī.* In regard to the spiritual experience they have, there is no difference at all. An important distinction that deserves attention here is the one that is made between the first three types of *arhats* on the one hand and the rest, on the other. The first three are the Tīrtaṅkara type and the rest, the non-Tīrtaṅkara type. The distinction between the two is that the former is capable of preaching and propagating religious doctrines in order to guide the mundane souls immersed in the life of illusion, (his sermons are properly worded by the *gaṇadharas*) while the latter is not the propounder of religious faith or principles, but silently enjoys the sublimity of mystical experience.[3] It is well-known that

[3] K. C. Sogani, *op. cit.*, p. 199

the number of Tīrtaṅkaras for every age is believed to be only twenty-four. This need not be a discouraging factor for the spiritual aspirants because it is maintained that the next higher stage of the *siddha* is considered to be possible even for the non-Tīrthaṅkaras.

The *Arhat* is considered to be the ideal saint and the perfect *guru*. He is also designated as *Paramātman* or god. From the distinct view-point that Jainism takes in regard to the description of godhead, it is natural for us to expect that the *arhats* are not enpowered to do any favour to those who worship them. As Upadhye points out : "Neither *arhat* nor *siddha* has on him the responsibility of creating, supporting or destroying the world. The aspirant receives no boons, no favours and no curses from him by way of gifts from the divinity. The aspiring souls pray to him, worship him and meditate on him as an example, as a model, as an ideal that they too might reach the same condition."[4] It is thus held that worshipping *arhats* is effective inasmuch as it creates confidence in the devotees that spiritual advancement and perfection will be possible for them too.

With all the attempts at describing the nature of the *arhat*, as Sogani points out, the essence of the *arhat* cannot be completely exhausted in conceptual and rational terms. The luminous aspect of the *arhat* eludes a complete comprehension of it in purely rational or ethical terms. Though sometimes purely negative descriptions are attempted, they all point to some experience which is positive, which can be had only through pure meditation or contemplation.[5]

Siddha : This stage represents the trans-empirical state. The *siddha* is one who has escaped from the causal plane, who has escaped from the teeth of *karma*. The *siddha* is described as not being the product of anything nor producing anything.[6] Since he has escaped from the shackles of *karma* altogether, he is completely independent of all external objects. Naturally therefore there is no question of his experiencing either pleasure or pain. His is a state of infinite, pure and unlimited bliss.

4 Cited in K. C. Sogani, *op. cit.*, p. 199
5 See K. C. Sogani, *Ibid.*, p. 203
6 *Pañcāstikāya*, 36

The acquisition of siddhāhood is synonymous with attaining *nirvāṇa*,[7] where negatively speaking there is no pain, nor pleasure, nor any *karmas* nor auspicious and inauspicious *dhyānas*, nor any thing such as annoyance, obstruction, death, birth, senses, calamity, delusion, wonder, sleep, desire and hunger and, where, positively speaking, there is perfect intuition, knowledge, bliss, potency, immateriality and existence.[8] The *Ācārāṅga* describes the *siddha* stage thus : "All sounds recoil thence where speculation has no room, nor does the mind penetrate there. The liberated is without body, without resurrection, without contact of matter ; he is not feminine, nor masculine, nor neuter; he perceives, he knows, but there is no analogy ; its essence is without form ; there is no condition of the unconditioned."[9]

With the attainment of the *nirvāṇa* stage, the *jīva's* aspirations for freeing itself from the malignant influence of *ajīva* are realized. It reaches the top of the universe and there is no fall from it. It shines forth as a glorious example of what has been achieved by one *jīva* and what can and ought to be achieved by the other *jīvas*. The description of the six-fold monastic order is thus a description of the *jīva* in its various stages of perfection, institutionally considered.

[7] *Niyamasāra,* 183
[8] *Ibid.*, 178-181
[9] I. 5. 6. 3. 4

29

Doctrine of Gunasthana

THE Jaina philosophers have analysed the various stages through which spiritual perfection can be attained. They refer to *fourteen* stages through which the purity of soul—purity of existence and consciousness—is experienced. These stages are referred to as *guṇasthānas*. Sometimes the term 'states of virtue' is made use of to refer to the various steps through which the *jīva* ascends the ladder of life and reaches the summit of perfection. The temr 'states of virtue' is acceptable provided it is understood not in the limited sense of ethical or moral character-building, but in the deeper sense of aiming at and realizing spiritualization in one's life.

In terms of the *ratna-traya* doctrine : ultimately, spiritual perfection consists in the individual soul developing *samyagdarśana*, *samyagjñāna* and *samyagcāritra*. Every soul has the potentiality to 'get at' all the three 'gems', but the potentiality becomes actualized gradually and, what is more important, through the *individual's own initiative*. We shall outline the various stages of the spiritual journey.

Stage 1 : *Mithyā-dṛṣṭi-guṇasthāna* : In one sense this is not actually a stage in the soul's journey towards perfection. It represents the bottom-most step in the ladder. The soul in this stage is characterized by spiritual blindness. The individual's thought is devoid of any idea of truth and goodness. The stage represents the superstitious stage in that the individual is easily susceptible to believing as true any superficially attractive idea that is suggested. There is here a positive belief in wrong knowledge and *darśanāva-*

raṇa karma is responsible for the individual's repudiating truth and accepting untruth as the gospel. In short, this is the stage of the wrong believer.

Stage 2 : *Sāsādana-samyagdṛṣṭi-guṇasthāna* : This is the stage when the soul has slightly tasted right belief. The stage is normally considered not as an evolution from the first stage but as a result of a fall from a higher stage. The stage is considered to be a halting stage for those souls which have slipped down from a higher stage, especially from that stage where, after the first enlightenment, passions overtake the soul.

Here it should be emphasized that the Jaina philosophers, very much like the Hindu philosophers, believed that a teacher (*guru*) initiates the individual on to the tradition. The Jaina philosophers, however, point out that sometimes it happens that the individual gets suddenly awakened to the faith in the tradition. Such cases are explained as cases of the individuals who, though they had received initiation in a previous birth, had failed to follow it and forgotten all about it, and that in a later birth there is the revival of the memory.

The Jaina philosophers have not failed to notice that there is every likelihood of the individual slipping down the ladder due to intervening passions. In case the individual slips down to the first stage, he has to begin the spiritual ascent afresh.

Stage 3 : *Miśra-guṇasthāna* : This stage represents the oscillating experience of the individual. The oscillation referred to is between right faith and wrong faith. The mind is constantly agitated and it is not able to settle down to complete faith. Even while entering faith, loss of faith occurs, but once again the mind swings back to faith. The stage of conflict naturally cannot last long since the individual makes conscious attempts at getting over the conflict-situation.

Stage 4 : *Avirata samyagdṛṣṭi guṇasthāna* : In this stage the mind settles down to entertaining right thoughts and hence right faith. This is a significant stage in spiritual evolution because there is a definite indication that right knowledge and conduct are at least conceptually visualized and there is every possibility of the individual putting his theory of truth and conduct into practice.

In this stage, even though right faith is entertained, the individual becomes unrestrained in regard to his sense organs. The reason for the absence of self-control in this stage is that the right faith which has been attained is due to only one of the three types of *karma* being overcome. These are : complete subsidence of the vision-deluding *karma* (*aupaśamika*), subsidence-cum-dissociation of the relevant *karma* (*kṣayopaśamika*) and the annihilation of the life-long passions and the three types of vision-deluding *karma* (*kṣayika-samyagdṛṣṭi*). Unless all the three are accomplished, self-control cannot be attained and unless self-control is gained the next stage cannot be attained.

Stages 5, 6 & 7 : Deśavirata samyagdṛṣṭi guṇasthāna, Pramatta saṁyata guṇasthāna & Apramatta saṁyata guṇasthāna : These refer to the struggles that go on between the individual's will which tries to conquer the sensual desires and the sense organs which constantly try to pull the individual down. Success is naturally to be gained only gradually. The first stage where there is only partial success signifies that there is a spiritual disposition and though there is earnestness and effort on the part of the individual, he meets only with partial success in the battle. In the next stage success is almost achieved. It seems as if full control has been gained by the individual, but the impulses have still got some sway over him. Distraction is the result and self-mastery is not complete. Thus in this stage also the full power of the soul does not come to the fore and it can well be described as a stage of spiritual inertia (*pramatta-saṁyata*). In the third stage the individual is crowned with complete success, he gains real mastery over himself. The spirit has after all conquered the body. Spiritual inertia which characterized the previous stage has been overcome. This stage is considered to be a critical one in that the individual, from this stage of his evolution can either reach absolute perfection or only relative perfection. Absolute perfection is attainable by thoroughly annihilating the evil effects of *karma* and the path-way to this is referred to as *kṣapaka śreṇi*. Relative perfection refers to the mere passifying of the kārmic influence on the purity of the soul and this is referred to as *upaśama śreṇi*.

Stage 8 : Nivṛtti bādara samparāya guṇasthāna : This is characterized by the soul acquiring a rare psychical force which can be made use of in the subjugation and eradication of *karma*. Due to the purity of the soul at this stage it is even capable of shortening the duration and weakening the intensity of the *karmas* which had a binding effect on it previously. There is a contact with fresh *karmas* but the duration and intensity of the fresh *karmas* contacted are limited. The individual in this stage is filled with confidence, for, never before has he experienced such strength of will and such powers which are at his command.

Stages 9 & 10 : Anivṛtti bādara samparāya guṇasthāṇa & Sūkṣma samparāya guṇasthāna : These represent the stages of 'spiritual warfare' and the new weapon with which the individual is equipped is made use of. In the first stage there is mainly a fight against the gross emotions and crude impulses (*anivṛtti bādara*). In the next stage the battle is waged against emotions and passions (*sūkṣma*) which are experienced by the individual in a subtle form.

Stage 11 : Upaśānta kaṣāya vītarāga chadmastha guṇasthāna : This stage of spiritual evolution witnesses the total suppression of the passions and to this extent the individual has succeeded in getting rid of the evil influences of *karma*. He is free from attachment (*vītarāga*). Yet there is always the danger of the recurrence of the passions and emotions, and hence also the kārmic influence being exerted again. From the point of view of *upaśama śreṇi* this stage represents the peak of the summit.

Stage 12 : Kṣīṇa kaṣāya vītarāga chadmastha guṇasthāna : Annihilation of kārmic influence is effectively achieved in this stage and this represents the end of the journey represented by the *jīva* treading on the steps of the *kṣīṇaka śreṇi*. This stage represents the peak of the summit of annihilated passions (*kṣiṇa kasāya*).

Stage 13 : Sayogi kevali guṇasthāna : In the last instant of the previous stage, the soul becomes completely free from the four obscuring *karmas*, viz., *jñānāvaraṇa*, *darṣanāvaraṇa*. *vedanīya* and *mohanīya karmas*. *Kevala-jñāna* is attained in this stage. Still the activity of the body, mind and speech continues (*sayogi*). The soul is not free from the four *aghāti karmas*, viz., *āyus*, *nāma*, *gotra* and *antarāya karmas*. When the *āyus karmas* get exhausted, the effects of the other *karmas* also cease. Before the next stage is reached all activities come to a stop.

Stage 14 : Ayogi kevali guṇasthāna : This is the stage of complete freedom. In this stage the individual transcends all traces of imperfection and he enjoys purity of consciousness. This is the consummation stage of getting the right faith, right knowledge and right conduct. The truth of existence is realized in its completeness by the individual. The stage is considered to be a motionless one and is of a very short duration. At the end of this period, unembodied emancipation is attained.

30

The Anuvrata Movement

THE *Aṇuvrata* movement, started by the great Jaina saint Ācārya Tulasi in Rajasthan in 1949 is a positive evidence to the vitality of the Jaina religion as also to the presence of the life and world affirming elements in it. It contains, therefore, the vows and beliefs traditional to Jainism but the presentation itself reflected the corruption of man and society that had come about at the time the movement was thought of and launched (which still continues) and the immediate necessity of re-building of character that was felt at the time. Ācārya Tulasi believes that the aim of Jainism (from an empirical standpoint) is the development of the individual' scharacter.

He emphasizes that the ills of society automatically get cured by means of the process of self-purification and self-control. From this point of view he maintains that the view sometimes expressed, viz., that the function of religion is the control of society is incorrect. By developing the character of the individual the level of social morality is made to go up but the latter is not the main aim of religion. Explaining his point of view regarding religion in general and Jainism in particular, he writes : "A devotee at the time of initiation takes a holy vow that for the good of self he accepts five *mahāvratas* as his discipline throughout life. The end of a *vrata* is freedom from bondage. Its incidental result is also the control of society, but this is not the main consequence of it."[1] Accordingly

[1] Ācārya Tulāsi, *Can Intellect Comprehend Religion?* (Churu : Adarsh Sahitya Sangh, 1969), p. 18

he thinks that to adopt religion for glorification here on earth or to practise it as a preparing ground for a 'better future' in the next—both are wrong. The significance of religion for the individual soul is such that when practised for the sake of self-purification beneficial results in this world (in society) and in the next accrue automatically. Thus the insistence on the importance of the individual in religion is not born out of disregard for society or concern for a world to come but out of the conviction that when the individual is purified society gets purified as a result. Such a view of religion explains also the non-sectarian nature of the *Aṇuvrata* movement.

At the time the movement was initiated, Ācārya Tulasi himself was considered to be an orthodox philosopher and as the leader of the Jaina sect. Since the name of the movement also was derived from the Jaina tradition it looked as if the Ācārya was only trying to propagate a sectarian religion, though with a new key. The question of a different nomenclature which would not smack of a narrow derivation from a particular tradition, — however rich the tradition itself may be—was considered but it was found that no other name would reflect the spirit of the movement. The Ācārya was more keen on an action-oriented movement than on giving to the world an imposing nomenclature to a philosophy of individual regeneration. The term *aṇuvrata* was considered to represent the conviction that small vows can effect big changes. The movement was however named *Aṇuvrata Saṅgha*, to start with, with the modification of it as *Aṇuvrata movement* coming later on. The base of the movement is ultimately to be traced to a nine-point programme and a thirteen-point scheme which were experimentally tried and accepted by twenty-five thousand people.[2] The nine-point programme was : (1) not to think of committing suicide; (2) not to use wine and other intoxicating drugs; (3) not to take meat and eggs; (4) not to indulge in a big theft; (5) not to gamble; (6) not to indulge in illicit and unnatural intercourse; (7) not to give any evidence to favour a false case and untruth ; (8) not to adulterate things nor to sell

[2] See Muni Nathmal, *Ācārya Tulasi* : *His Life and Philosophy* (Churu : Ādarsh Sahitya Sangh, 1968), p. 67

imitation products as genuine and (9) not to be inaccurate in weight and measure. The thirteen-point scheme was : (1) not to kill intentionally moving, innocent creatures ; (2) not to commit suicide ; (3) not to take wine ; (4) not to eat meat ; (5) not to steal ; (6) not to gamble ; (7) not to depose falsely ; (8) not to set fire to buildings or materials out of malice or under temptation ; (9) not to indulge in illicit and unnatural intercourse ; (10) not to visit prostitutes ; (11) not to smoke and not to make use of intoxicating drugs ; (12) not to take food at night and (13) not to prepare food for *sādhus*.

The *Aṇuvrata Saṅgha* incorporated in its programme eighty-four vows. The institution of the *Saṅgha* being in its infant stage and being also motivated towards incorporating the actual experiences of the public for whose benefit it was intended, was flexible and open enough to accept some changes. Five years after its initiation the outline of the entire movement was changed and, in response to the suggestion that the term *Aṇuvrata movement* was a better one than *Aṇuvrata Saṅgha*, the Ācārya changed the name. The preference for the new name was expressed on the ground that it indicated a broader aim and outlook than the old one. The movement was not confined to India merely and the response it evoked in a leading American weekly is worth mentioning here. Under the caption *Atomic Boss* it wrote : "Like some men at various other places here is an Indian, lean, thin and short-statured but with shining eyes who is very much worried at the present state of the world. He is Tulasi, aged 34, the preceptor of the Jaina Terapantha which is a religious organisation having faith in non-violence. Ācārya Tulasi had founded the Aṇuvrati Saṁgha in 1949 . . . When he should have succeeded in making all Indians undertake the vows, his plan is also to convert the rest of the world so as to adopt the life of a 'vrati' !"[3]

The founder of the movement himself declares that the attitude of the movement towards other religions is one of good-will and tolerance. He points out that since the basic principles emphasized in it are universal, followers of any religion can become its members and subscribe to its ideals. An objection to the description of the Aṇuvrata movement as universal in character and scope is anti-

[3] *Time* of New York, dated May 15, 1959

cipated and answered by the Ācārya. The objection is that the term *aṇuvrata* is taken from the Jaina precepts which require the possession of right vision (*sāmyagdarśana*) from the *aṇuvrati*. Since *samyagdarśana* refers to a comprehension of the Jaina view of life, there is no scope for religious tolerance and universal outlook in an *aṇuvrati*. The Ācārya's reply is that since a non-violent vision adequately describes the scope and philosophy of *aṇuvrata*, it is quite in keeping with the spirit of Jaina thought and culture to make use of the term in a slightly different sense. In substance the Ācārya's view is that the term is extended to engulf a similar ideology discernible in all religions by a deeper interpretation of a traditional concept.[4]

Here it is worthwhile considering two leading criticisms against the Jaina view of *ahiṁsā* and *aparigraha* since it gives the necessary perspective from which the *Aṇuvrata movement* can be understood. The Jaina view that ultimately non-violence should pervade every sphere of life and light up all the other virtues is pointed out as expecting far too much from its followers. Even a moment's thought will reveal that in any system of ethics it is most essential that some one principle is posited as central to all and considered as a co-ordinating and regulative value. We have to add, however, that the primacy given to the principle of *ahiṁsā* is not born out of a necessity to have *any* one value as the 'co-ordinator'. The reason lies much deeper and can be gathered by recapitulating the doctrine of continuity of consciousness that we find in Jainism. In brief, the doctrine signifies that if the *jīvas* are in various stages of evolution towards perfection (getting freed from the *ajīvas*) no one *jīva*—at whatever higher stage it may be—has any right to interfere with the spiritual prospects of any other *jīva*—at whatever lower stage of evolution it may be. In the Jaina theory we find the attitude of *reverence for life* clearly comprehended and systematically treated.

The emphasis laid on non-possession along with non-violence is even more severely criticised on the ground that expecting the most severe observance of the principle is too unrealistic to be of any value in having an influence over the adherents of the faith. The severe standard set by the Jaina philosophers is no doubt evident from the unambiguous language they use to explain the seriousness

[4] *op. cit.*, p. 28

of the state of bondage, but certainly they have not been unrealistic about the ability of the common man to put the principles to practice. Extremely strict observance of the five principles of *ahiṁsā*, *satya*, *asteya*, *brahmacarya* and *aparigraha* is referred to as observance of the great vows (*mahāvratas*) and it is more often than not forgotten that there are five lesser vows (*aṇuvratas*) accepted in the Jaina tradition. The *aṇuvratas* are prescribed for the house-holder who has not yet renounced the world, who, however should start practising the virtues *in spirit*.

Accordingly, the *aṇuvratas* do not differ in kind from the *mahāvratas*, but laxity is allowed in their observance, keeping in view the limitations of the house-holder. It is obvious that the prescription of *aṇuvratas* for observance by the house-holder is based on the psychological insight of the Jaina philosophers that with the various obligations that a house-holder owes to others in society—both within and outside his house-hold—it is not possible to observe the *vratas* scrupulously.

The *Aṇuvrata movement* as the prescription of the *aṇuvrâtas* is also based on the necessity to re-orient the thought and behaviour of the common man towards the ideal of non-violence and non-possession. Whereas a distinction is drawn between the house-holder and the ascetic by prescribing the *aṇuvratas* to the house-holder and *mahāvratas* to the ascetic in the traditional Jaina thought, in the *Aṇuvrata movement* the distinction is drawn between the beginner, the middling and the advanced types of *aṇuvratis*, respectively referred to as *praveśaka aṇuvrati*, *aṇuvrati* and *viśiṣṭa aṇuvrati*.

In the traditional Jaina thought non-violence prescribed is considered purely in the context of spiritual evolution and from the point of view of reverence for life in whichever form it is manifest in the universe. In the *Aṇuvrata movement* emphasis on spiritual evolution is not replaced by social considerations, but the beneficial results for society are clearly envisaged. The movement was born when the situation in the world characterized by extreme violence, greed and hatred was pondered over. Though the social conditions were analysed, the solution given was not purely in terms of *ordering about* the reconstitution of social relations or introducing legislative changes in the institutions. The Ācārya's standpoint is clear from his words. He writes : "Man has become emaciated as a result of the shocks of war and cold war, and the competition in weapons and missiles. He has no alternative but to purify the internal self. If there is no change in it, complete dissolution of the world is not far off. This movement prescribes that man should have faith not in weapons but in non-violence. Instead of giving primacy to worldly progress he should awaken his spiritual consciousness."[5] "The economists say that its (society's) main problem is greater productivity. Superficially viewed, the problem seems to have been solved to a certain extent. But I do not think that it can be solved as long as we are overgreedy. Its unexceptionable solution is self-control. A devoted life imparts peace to us and also at the same time offers us a solution to economic problems."[6]

In regard to non-possession : the traditional emphasis on it was a result of regarding it as promoting the conditions under which attachment and all the attendant evils are cast off. The modern movement does not overlook the evil influence of non-soul (*ajīva*) on the soul (*jīva*) in the absence of purity of character in the realm of possession even. Non-possession is considered to be a "form of non-violence which has no expectation of objects from others."[7] Hence the vow is considered to effect limitation of one's desires. The Ācārya emphatically points out : "Social regulations can be an effective check on possessions, but not on human desires. This *vrata* means the control of possessions, through the control of desires."[8]

It is evident then that the *Aṇuvrata movement* emphasizes the twin-principles of non-violence and non-possession as basic to reorienting the other values and to reconstructing society. Emphasizing the need for self-analysis and self-purification even in the modern world, the Ācārya writes : "It is true that man's external powers have increased manifold, but it is no less true that internal strength has considerably reduced. As the inner states of mind grow vicious, situations get complicated. The root of diseases lies in the deterioration in the qualities of the inner self. Man has been dazzled by external glitter. He has not been able to find an answer

[5] *Ibid.*, p. 27
[6] *Ibid.*, p. 29
[7] *Ibid.*, p. 21
[8] *Ibid.*

to the question whether the modern age is one of development or decadence."[9] It should not, however, be forgotten that the aims of the movement can be realized only by following the spirit of all the five 'vows'.

We may then conclude without contradiction that the significance of the *Aṇuvrata movement* as a cure for the evils of the present day lies in its being the application of the essential Jaina philosophy of the five vows to the changed time with suitable modifications, and also in its approach to the whole problem of peace and unity by suggesting that the immense potentialities that each individual has for promoting social unity can be actualized by developing inner harmony and regulated spiritual evolution.

[9] *Ibid.*, p. 29

Bibliography

A History of Indian Philosophy, Vol. I (S.N. Dasgupta, Cambridge University Press, 1963)
Ācārāṅga
Ācārya Tulasi : His Life and Philosophy (Muni Nathmal, Adarsh Sahitya Sangh, Churu, 1968)
Ādi Purāṇa
Antakṛddaśāḥ
Anuttaraupapādikadaśāḥ
Archaeological Survey of India Reports, Vol. III
Āvaśyaka-niryukti (Bhadrabāhu)
Baudhāyana Dharma-Sūtra
Bhagavatī-Sūtra
Brahadāraṇyaka Upaniṣad
Buddhist Logic (Th. Stcherbastsky, Leningrad, 1930)
Christian and Hindu Ethics (S. C. Thakur, George Allen & Unwin Ltd., London, 1969)
Chāndogya Upaniṣad
Daśavaikālika-niryukti (Bhadrabāhu)
Dravya-saṅgraha & Commentary
Encyclopaedia of Religion and Ethics, Vols. 11, 12 & 22
Epigraphica Indica, I
Ethical Doctrines in Jainism (K. C. Sogani, Jaina Samskriti Samrakshaka Sangha, Sholapur, 1967)
Gautama Dharma-Sūtra
Gommaṭasāra

Hinduism and Buddhism, Vol. I (C. Eliot, Routledge & Kegan Paul Ltd., London, 1962)

History of Indian Philosophy, Vol. I (U. Mishra, Tirabhukti Publications, Allahabad 1967)

Indian Antiquary, Vols. II, VII, IX, XVII, XIV, & XX

Indian Philosophy (S. Radhakrishnan, George Allen & Unwin Ltd., London)

Jaina Psychology (M.L. Mehta, Jaina Dharma Pracharak Samiti, 1955)

Jaina Sūtras, pt. I (H. Jacobi, trans., Motilal Banarsidass, 1964)

Jaina Theories of Reality and Knowledge (Y.J. Padmarajiah, Jain Sahitya Vikas Mandal, Bombay, 1963)

Jaina View of Life (T.G. Kalghatgi, Jaina Saṁskṛti Samrakshaka Sangha, Sholapur, 1969)

Jainism in North India (C. J. Shah, Longman Green & Co., London, 1932)

Jñāta-Sūtra

Kalpa-Sūtra

Karmagrantha

Kaṭha Upaniṣad

Nandi-Sūtra

Niyamasāra (Kundakunda)

Nyāyāvatāra vṛtti

Outlines of Indian Philosophy (M. Hiriyanna, George Allen & Unwin Ltd., London, 1957)

Outlines of Jaina Philosophy (M.L. Mehta, Jain Mission Society, Bangalore, 1954)

Pañcāstikāya (Kundakunda)

Parīkṣā-mukha-sūtra (Māṇikyanandi)

Philosophies of India (Zimmer, Routledge & Kegan Paul, London, 1953)

Pramāṇa-Mīmāṁsa (Hemacandra) & Commentary.

Pramāṇanayatattvālokālaṅkāra (Vādideva)

Pravacanasāra

Principles of Psychology (William James, London, 1946)

Psychological Principles (James Ward)

Reals in the Jaina Metaphysics (H.S. Bhattacharya, The Seth Santi Das Khetsy Charitable Trust, Bombay, 1966)

Reign of Religion in Indian Philosophy (R. Nagaraja Sarma)

Religion of Ahiṁsā (A. Chakravarti, Ratanchand Hirachand, Bombay, 1957)
Ṣaddarśanasamuccaya
Sanmati-tarka-prakaraṇa (Siddhasena)
Sarvārthasiddhi (Devānandi)
Ṣatkhaṇdāgama (Puṣpadanta)
Sthānāṅga-Sūtra
Studies in Jaina Philosophy (N. Tatia, Jaina Cultural Research Society, Banaras, 1951)
Studies in Jainism (Jina Vijaya Muni, Jaina Sahitya Samsodhaka Studies, Ahmedabad, 1946)
Syādvādamañjarī (Hemacandra)
Tattvārtha-śloka vārttika (Vidyānanda)
Tattvārtha-Sūtra (Umāswāmi)
Tattvārtha-Sūtra bhāṣya (Umāswāmi)
Upāsakadaśāḥ
Uttarādhyayana-Sūtra
Viśeṣāvaśyaka-bhāṣya (Jīnabhadra)
Viśiṣṭādvaita (P.N. Srinivasachari)
Viṣṇupurāṇa (H.H. Wilson, trans.)

Index